"A lifesaving and life-affirming text, *Community as Rebellion* offers us the trenchant analysis and fearless strategy radical scholar-activists have long needed. But Lorgia García Peña's intervention is especially valuable at this moment, as we collectively consider how our most important social institutions might be reimagined beyond the strongholds of white supremacy, heteropatriarchy, and racial capitalism more broadly." —**Angela Y. Davis**, coauthor of *Abolition. Feminism. Now.*

"*Community as Rebellion* is a must-read for anyone serious about confronting institutional racism, sexism, and elitism. Lorgia García Peña, one of her generation's most brilliant scholar-activists, challenges us to confront academia as a 'colonial and colonizing' space as the first step toward resistance and transformation. Her own experiences undergird her analysis and serve as a powerful call to action." —**Barbara Ransby**, author of *Eslanda: The Large and Unconventional Life of Mrs. Paul Robeson*

"Lorgia García Peña is one of the few courageous and brilliant intellectuals grounded in rigorous and visionary grassroots education. This pedagogical guide for genuine freedom struggles is so badly needed in our neofascist times!" —**Cornel West**, author of *Race Matters*

"Unflinching, brilliant, and absolutely necessary. In these pages, Lorgia García Peña shares her experiences, and those of others, to reflect on what it means to be 'the stranger' in academia: that sole symbol for diversity that still remains an outsider. Unwavering in its clarity and compassion, this powerful book reminds us that true belonging comes from actively building communities unafraid to center care and rebellion. Everyone should read this." —**Maaza Mengiste**, author of *The Shadow King*

"'What does it mean to teach for freedom?' Dr. García Peña asks and boldly beckons us toward its practice across the policed borders of discipline, nation, theoretical traditions, and entrenched racial categories. A capacious thinker, rigorous researcher, brilliant activist, and path-breaking scholar, Dr. García Peña calls on us, as she writes, to 'mind the historical gaps' for long-subjugated stories and alerts us to the ways these gaps have been historically mined in extractive ways in the service of colonial projects and neoliberal calls for diversity. Her astonishing work gathers us under its broad canopy to plot and persevere toward communal rebellion and renewal." —**Deborah Paredez**, author of *Year of the Dog*

"With characteristic clarity, courage, and conviction, Lorgia García Peña draws on her remarkable history as an engaged scholar and committed activist to demonstrate the necessity of living in community and accompanying others as keys to both personal liberation and social transformation." —**George Lipsitz**, author of *The Possessive Investment in Whiteness*

"*Community as Rebellion* is partly an incisive and deeply personal exposé of the neoliberal university and its racializing and patriarchal practices of denigrating women of color scholars while extracting their intellectual, administrative, and emotional labor. But it is, above all, a mandate to transform higher education that begins with recognizing our mutual obligations to each other and to the world we study, extending 'community' beyond the ivory tower, and co-creating with our students new, autonomous intellectual spaces. Lorgia García Peña wrote this book not from a dream or an abstract theory but from building rebel communities for over a decade. She knows that there can be no free education without freedom."—**Robin D. G. Kelley**, author of *Freedom Dreams: The Black Radical Imagination*

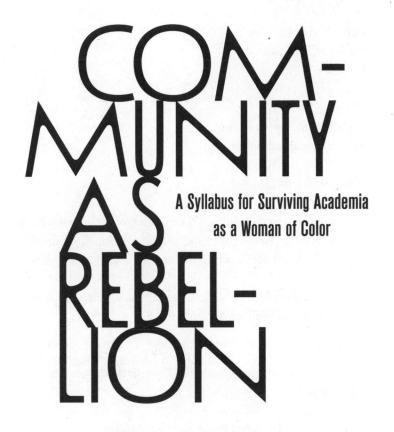

COM- MUNITY AS REBEL- LION

A Syllabus for Surviving Academia as a Woman of Color

Lorgia García Peña

Haymarket Books
Chicago, Illinois

Published in 2022 by
Haymarket Books
P.O. Box 180165
Chicago, IL 60618
773-583-7884
www.haymarketbooks.org
info@haymarketbooks.org

ISBN: 978-1-64259-692-2

Distributed to the trade in the US through Consortium Book Sales
and Distribution (www.cbsd.com) and internationally through
Ingram Publisher Services International (www.ingramcontent.com).

This book was published with the generous support of Lannan
Foundation and Wallace Action Fund.

Special discounts are available for bulk purchases by organizations
and institutions. Please email info@haymarketbooks.org for more
information.

Cover artwork from *Fire* by Teresita Fernández.
Cover design by Rachel Cohen.

Printed in Canada by union labor.

Library of Congress Cataloging-in-Publication data is available.

10 9 8 7 6 5 4 3 2 1

To bell hooks, in memoriam

To the women of color whose backs have been my bridges

To my students, who made a home for me
in this barbed wire that is academia

CONTENTS

COURSE REQUIREMENTS

1. An open heart
2. A flexible mind
3. The desire to be part of the sum, rather than a single part
4. Patience

Recommended Aids

1. The company of friends
2. A warm beverage
3. A comfortable place to lie or sit
4. A sunny window

Further Reading

On Being Included, by Sara Ahmed

This Bridge Called My Back, edited by Gloria Anzaldúa and Cherríe Moraga

Levente no. yolayorkdominicanyork, by Josefina Báez

"Rethinking Radical Anti-Racist Feminist Politics in a Global Neoliberal Context," by Ochy Curiel, translated by Manuela Borzone and Alexander Ponomareff

Abolition. Feminism. Now. by Angela Y. Davis, Gina Dent, Erica R. Meiners, and Beth E. Richie

"Teaching Community: A Pedagogy of Hope," by bell hooks

Plantation Memories: Episodes of Everyday Racism, by Grada Kilomba

Sister Outsider: Essays and Speeches, by Audre Lorde

Feminism without Borders, by Chandra Talpade Mohanty

How We Get Free: Black Feminism and the Combahee River Collective, edited by Keeanga-Yamahtta Taylor

PREFACE

My family says I was born rebellious. As a child I grew accustomed to hearing people describe me as *malcriada* (uncivil), always making trouble, always speaking up when I was supposed to stay quiet. One of my first weapons of rebellion was my hair. I grew up in a predominantly Afro-descendant culture in which girls were expected to straighten our hair with chemicals and hot combs or otherwise groom it tight into submission. Mothers would be judged by the state of their little girls' hair. Therefore, all the little girls were socialized into the same ritual of making kinks and curls disappear to make ourselves "beautiful." From a very early age I refused these rituals, kicking and screaming every time someone tried (to no avail) to "tame" my hair. As soon as my mom styled my hair into five perfect (and extremely tight) coils, I would pull them out, letting my kinks fly wild. The kids would yell at me: "*¡Pajonúa, greñúa!*" (Dominican slang terms to describe a girl with messy, unruly, "bad" hair). The nuns at my school would discipline me, warn me that the future for rebellious children was hell. The nice aunties at church would entice me with pretty ribbons, showing me pictures of white children "looking pretty with their hair nicely tamed." Nothing worked.

In the 1970s Dominican Republic, having natural hair was akin to rebellion. Activist women who aligned with the socialist revolution would grow Afros or otherwise leave their kinks unconstrained. A common tactic of the repressive Joaquín Balaguer regime (1966–

1978) was to round up women with Afros and throw them in jail or shave off their hair in front of a crowd to teach them a lesson. Growing up in the 1980s and 1990s Dominican Republic, I was completely unaware of this violence; all I knew was I needed my hair to be free.

The summer I turned eleven, my mother, tired of dealing with my rebellious hair, sent me to my grandmother's with the task of "fixing that hair" once and for all. My grandmother and I walked to the local market to get coconut oil and cacao butter to make a concoction that would "soften my kinks" and make them "easier to manage." As we walked home together, we bumped into an old family friend, Doña Yolanda. She was a skinny lady with long, dark, shiny, and very straight hair, which she always wore in a ponytail. Upon laying her eyes on me, Doña Yolanda let out a loud gasp: "*¡Dios mío!* Is this Maritza's youngest?" She shook her head in disapproval, advising my grandmother, "Such a pretty girl, but that awful hair ruins her! You must do something about this, Altagracia. People are beginning to question your daughter. This child needs to be put in her place at once, or she will bring shame to your family!"

Doña Yolanda spoke as if I were not there, as if somehow my hair blocked my hearing. My grandmother nodded and sighed in silence. Neither woman looked at me. As we walked home in silence, I kept my eyes on the ground. Warm tears fell down my cheeks. I had grown accustomed to children teasing me at school. The constant scolding of the nuns didn't faze me; I didn't believe their threats. Until that moment, watching my grandmother sigh in what I perceived as shame and resignation, I realized my "bad" hair reflected on my entire family. I was filled with overwhelming shame.

When we arrived at the house, I broke our silence, the words streaming out: "I'll let you do my hair or cut it or whatever you want! I won't complain. I'm sorry I caused my family shame. I didn't mean to. I just don't like my hair constrained. It hurts my head. It makes me feel bad. It's not me. But I don't care. I will not complain,

I will let you tame it." I don't know what shocked my grandmother more, my words or my tears. She, too, began to cry.

She put our market bags on the floor and gently fluffed my hair, moving it away from my face. She took her time untangling the kinks and fluffing it up and out before guiding me to a small mirror my grandfather had hung on a mango tree in the yard for shaving. My hair was so big it didn't fit in the frame. We both laughed as she said, "Move back so you can see!" It was a sunny afternoon, and the light reflected on my reddish kinks as if they were on fire. My eyes, full of tears, stung from the reflection. I turned away and began to say I was sorry again, but my grandmother cupped my face in her hands, then turned me slowly back to the mirror. She stood behind me and asked me to look again. "I see your fire," she said, before adding, "Your hair is your weapon and your crown." And then, fluffing it up some more, "Let it roar!" I imagine she must have shared this with my mother and aunties, for there was no more talk in the family about taming my hair.

Rebellion, my mother tells me, is in my nature: "You were born a rebel," she always says whenever I share with her stories about the fights I take on at work and to support my students. She is now proud of my rebellious nature. When I ask her why exactly she thinks I was born rebellious, she tells me the story of how the riots of August 16 had made her go into early labor, "as if you wanted to come out fists up and join the rebels." Following austerity measures and a general strike, people had taken to the streets of Santo Domingo, burning tires, throwing rocks, and confronting the police. My mother recalls being at her desk, packing up to go home to safety when her water broke: "It was too soon!" She was rushed to the hospital amid the chaos; my dad, who had joined the protesters, was nowhere to be found. As she got to the hospital in the city center ready to labor, I switched positions, head up and my legs crisscrossed, refusing to come out on demand. My mother, who had already birthed three children, could not believe my acrobatics. "I just knew I was in for trouble with this one," she recalls, laughing as she tells the story time and time again. "After three children, this one, the last one, came *como le dio la gana* (when and how she wanted), and I had no say in it. She was born a rebel."

As much as I enjoy hearing my birth story, I disagree with my mom. I was not born rebellious; I was nurtured into rebellion. My caregivers, my grandma and aunties, not only allowed it; they fostered it. They saw a small flame in my eyes, and they fueled it, with care, with warmth, and at times, with fury. It was their *community* that made my rebellion possible.

This book is both *una ofrenda* (an offering) to community and a call to rebellion. It comes out of a profound desire to honor the women that have made my life—as I have chosen to live it, in freedom and rebellion—possible. Women in both my blood and chosen family, ancestors, and friends, women I never met and women whose paths have crossed with mine. My writing comes from a place of deep gratitude and humility as I recognize all that I am as the result of a collective process of becoming that is informed by communal knowledge and shared imaginings. I am my mother's dreams fulfilled, my grandmother's vengeance realized, patriarchy's worst nightmare, a testament to the power of anticolonial resistance. I am all *they*—those who stole lands and enslaved people—were afraid of and more; rebellion is my birthright. This book is an altar of words, onto which to lay collective hopes for the possibility of radical dreams, for redress, restitution, reparation, and triumph.

I began to write *Community as Rebellion* as a letter to my students in early spring 2019. After attending an academic conference in 2018 in which my friends and fellow scholars of Dominican studies Sharina Maillo-Pozo and Elizabeth Manley and I felt dismissed and silenced, we decided to put together a symposium on the future of Dominican studies that would center the work of young scholars in the field. Five months later, "Global Dominicanidades" took place in Cambridge, Massachusetts. The one-day event convened dozens of young scholars, most of them women of color, pairing them with senior scholars in the field to create an environment of support and mentorship that acknowledged the challenges traditional conference settings have posed for so many of us women, people of color (POC), and queer scholars working in contradiction to hegemonic Eurocentric knowledge. We shared our work, provided feedback and support to each other, and most importantly, built a network and a community where we felt safe to rebel. As I reflected on the day, and as emails of gratitude kept pouring in, I began to write these pages. It was clear that the space Sharina, Beth, and I had created was more than a work event. We had opened a space from which *another* way of imagining the academy and the university is possible; our community contradicted the violence so many of us experience in our institutions. I wanted more.

For the almost two decades since I first began my academic path as a PhD student at the University of Michigan in 2003, I had been trying to make sense of my place in academia and the university as an Afro Latinx woman of immigrant background whose work was firmly grounded in knowledge and stories that have been subjugated by traditional university programs and fields. My experiences of discomfort and unbelonging in these predominantly white and highly elitist university spaces have been formative to who I am as a scholar, teacher, and mentor, and to how I move in the space that is both my job and an important part of my life.

For years I looked upon my unbelonging as a burden, as something to overcome in order to succeed. It is now a badge of honor: my unbelonging to the academy is as natural as my hair. It is a sign of all that must end for all of us to live full lives: racism, inequality, colonial structures, patriarchy, homophobia. As I realized the beauty that is my discomfort within the academy, I also yearned to create conditions of rebellion and freedom for the students I serve and for the new generation of colleagues I am honored to support. But as I shared these experiences and thoughts publicly, in multiple spaces within and beyond the university, it also became clear that these challenges are not unique to academia. Those of us who are made to unbelong experience the violence of exclusion everywhere. My unbelonging to the university comes from the structures of colonialism and racism that continue to shape all our institutions to date—the nation, our schools, our justice system. They are ingrained in the fabric of our society; therefore, to change, we need more than inclusion and diversity; we need revolution and rebirth. We need to start anew from a place in which the lives and experiences of people who have been silenced and excluded are centered.

Global Dominicanidades Conference, Harvard University, 2019

So I sat down to write a letter—a rant, really—to my students, to women and queer-identifying scholars of color, whose path would be similar to mine. I wrote as if my words could conjure their suffering, as if these words could be an antidote to that suffering. My hope is that the lessons I have learned over the last two decades in academia will bring us together in community, that they might accompany us on our path and make us feel our power. The stories shared throughout this book are thus shared with the knowledge that other ways are possible and with the conviction that possibility lies precisely in community. This book is then a very personal attempt to hold us, to gently move us closer to a mirror in which our fire is collectively reflected back to us, unleashing our community as rebellion.

1.

COURSE OBJECTIVE

On Being "The One"

> *Whiteness can be a situation we have or are in; when we can name that situation (and even make jokes about it) we recognize each other as strangers to the institution and find in that estrangement a bond....* We also want there to be more than one; we want not to be the one.
>
> —**Sara Ahmed,** *On Being Included: Racism and Diversity in Institutional Life* (emphasis added)

Soon after I was hired as assistant professor of Latinx studies, my department, Romance Languages and Literatures, was presented with what in the university we refer to as a "line," the opportunity to hire a full-time tenured or tenure-track professor. Tenure is an unusual system, unique to academia, that guarantees lifetime employment for faculty. It was designed to protect academic freedom and the intellectual work of faculty from external pressures, allowing for necessary but often controversial work to be done without fear of losing employment. In principle, tenure is supposed to protect professors who may criticize the government, shed light onto corrupt systems, or write about things that upset the structures of power. In reality, tenure functions as a reward, a sign of prestige vested upon the few faculty who are able to publish with prestigious presses, secure grants, and make an impact in their respective fields. Sadly, controversial scholars who rock the boat are, more often than not, denied tenure.[1] Tenure lines are coveted in academic departments, particularly in the humanities, for they potentially attract prestigious, well-established scholars who can build up the reputation of the department, support ongoing research agendas, advise students, and serve in the various administrative roles within the unit. Lines include tenured associate (midcareer level) and full professors (who have already found the holy grail), as well as assistant professors (usually newly minted PhDs who are working toward tenure).

Over the last two decades, tenure lines have become scant. According to the American Association of University Professors, only 21 percent of faculty are tenured.[2] The scarcity of tenure lines often causes rivalry between departments competing to obtain them. Following the neoliberal trend that affects all industries across the globe, the modern university is more concerned with cost reduction and the amassing of its endowment than with the production of knowledge and the well-being of its students. To maintain its neoliberal model, the university has significantly reduced its investment in full-time tenured professors, who cost more money and teach fewer courses as they are required or expected to conduct research and publish. Instead, universities employ low-paid graduate students and temporary, part-time teaching staff, such as adjunct professors and instructors, to teach the majority of the undergraduate courses. Even though adjuncts—like tenure-track and tenured professors—have doctoral degrees, they are paid less. Oftentimes adjuncts are paid a flat rate per course rather than a salary or a per hour rate. These flat rates amount to outrageously low wages, below the federal minimum, and put adjuncts' pay below the poverty line. Adjuncts are not offered health care benefits, research support, or at times even an office space. In the humanities and social sciences, temporary, contingent, or part-time employment is most common.[3]

In this dire employment climate in which humanities units such as Romance Languages, English, and Comparative Literatures, have been hemorrhaging student enrollment for decades all across the United States, hearing that our Romance languages and literatures department had received the approval of a tenured line was beyond exciting. During the faculty meeting, the chair asked all tenured and tenure-track faculty to offer our input to determine the specialization we should search for in the new hire. Romance languages departments are tricky, as they merge language learning and the literary and cultural studies of the Spanish-, French-, Italian-, and Portuguese-speaking world. The dynamics at play between, for example, scholars of France and specialists in Francophone Caribbean studies often mimic the very problematic colonial and racial tendencies that have shaped the unequal relationship between the European and US empires and the colonized sites. Think, for example, about the media portrayal of Haiti. The news cycle following the 2010 earthquake or, more recently, after the murder of Haitian president Jovenel Moïse in 2021, consistently referred to Haiti as the so-called "poorest country in the Western Hemisphere." By contrast, France is more often than not portrayed as a site of civility and culture, a country of beautiful, romantic cities, amazing wine, and great literature. The colonial structures that produce France as a site of civilization and Haiti as a hopeless location of underdevelopment are also at play in academic departments in ways that shape who is hired, what courses are taught, and which scholars are more valued, regardless of where students' interest lie. The biggest and most ridiculous irony of Romance languages departments is that those who do the most—usually professors who teach the literature of colonized countries—to serve the largest number of students also have the lowest salaries, are less likely to be tenured, and experience daily microaggressions from colleagues, administrators, and students. They are also more likely to be professors of color.

Over the past two decades, departments of Romance languages and literatures have been attracting Latinx students who, due to language and cultural affinity to Spanish and Portuguese, gravitate toward courses that focus on contemporary topics such as literatures of migration and postcolonial studies. At Harvard, where I worked for eight years in the Department of Romance Languages and Literatures, courses on Latin American and Latinx studies often sustained an enrollment of fifty-plus students per semester, while a course focusing on, let's say, the Italian Renaissance would have an enrollment of three students. At the University of Georgia where I also worked in the Romance Languages Department, our largest course was an introduction to Latinx literature—the course consistently enrolled 125 students per semester. Given this trend, and being the only Latinx studies scholar in the school's entire faculty of arts and sciences and one of only two Latinas teaching in the humanities at the time, when asked whom we should hire for the line, I raised both hands and insisted we prioritize hiring a Latinx studies scholar.[4] I suggested, too, that we make an effort to attract women candidates of color. Spoiler alert: the department instead chose to hire another expert in European literature, a white man.

Harvard, like many other elite schools throughout the United States, has significantly increased its admissions of students of color. By the beginning of fall 2021, 54 percent of undergraduate students identified as nonwhite; yet the number of faculty of color is still dismal. As a result, the few of us POC working in the university found ourselves overwhelmed by requests from students, administrators, and colleagues scrambling to serve the growing student of color population. Amid such inequality, it was logical to me that when presented with the opportunity to hire a full-time professor, we should prioritize the needs of the underserved student population. But, as I soon realized, logic and students' needs are not exactly how departmental decisions are made.

At the end of the meeting, a well-intentioned white senior colleague pulled me aside and told me that to protect my tenure, the department should not be hiring anyone else in Latinx studies, and especially not another Latina. They were sincere and well-meaning in their desire to protect me; they knew that in the eyes of the administration, there could be only one of us. I left the meeting perplexed, my hands shaking and sweating from the shock the encounter produced. I immediately summoned my support system—the other three women of color on the tenure track I knew at Harvard—to join me for a debriefing over dinner. While I was stunned about the realization that the university was actively making sure racial diversity among faculty did not grow beyond the representational (in opposition to the narrative of diversity and inclusion it professed), my colleagues were clear that having only "one of us" was indeed the modus operandi of the institution. Looking around the table, we were, as one of my friends put it, "a United Colors of Benetton ad," each of us exemplifying a different racialized ethnic minority. "Really? This is how they see us?" I asked, with a mixture of disbelief and disgust, as my friends laughed at my naivete.

My experience, while singular, is not unique. The pervasiveness of the "The One" model is all too familiar to women of color professionals working in competitive fields in the United States and other Global North countries. A Latina friend of mine once told me that her experience of working in a major financial institution had prepared her for war. We met in New York one afternoon, and as we walked along the pier, I asked her what it was like to be a Latina analyst at such a prestigious institution. I have to admit, I was in awe of her success and curious about what I presumed was a glamorous life. I had not yet told her about my experience of being The One. I remember she was eating an ice-cream cone and accidentally dropped it as I asked the question. She was laughing, maybe at having dropped the ice cream, maybe at my question, as she answered. But in my memory the laughter made her answer even more gutting:

> It's like being in a war zone. This job has conditioned me to receive so much violence, and to be triggered in so many ways, that I, sadly, can withstand the worst. Let me correct myself—working in my office *is* the worst; it is war. They spit at you without saliva. They question your intelligence, your right to be there. Someone actually told me once that they preferred [to hire] a different candidate, *pero*, you know, since I checked the diversity box, *they had to hire me. They had to.* I am convinced my colleagues resent and punish me just because I am not white.

My friend says I grew pale hearing her speak. "You're white like a ghost!" she said, which made her laugh even more. When I finally caught my breath, I asked her a question I have been asked whenever I speak publicly about the institutional violence academia inflicts on women of color: "Why don't you quit?" She rolled her eyes at me, before saying, "*Tú sabes por qué no* (you know why not). Why don't *you* leave Harvard? *Ajá*, and then what? Leave the next university and the next. You know they are all the same, right? For us, it is all the same shit." I smiled and rolled my eyes back at her. As two Latinas of working-class immigrant background, we shared a tacit knowledge: our careers are not only careers; they are jobs that support multigenerational members of our families. We cannot just quit, as we, contrary to some of our colleagues who have generational wealth, are the ones in our family who "made it." Financial constraints aside, the challenges of being "The One" for professional women of color transcends academia. Or as my friend put it, "I look around. Is it any better in other professions? Let's face it, unless I am making their beds or caring for their kids, I am going to be perceived as incompetent. There is nothing to do but fight. We gotta fight back. This is war."

The experiences of unbelonging that my dear friend and I lived through in completely different institutional spaces are sustained by white supremacy, by the belief that we, as minoritized women of color, do not belong; that we are only allowed to be part of these institutions because of our race and gender rather than despite them; that we are the "diversity hires." This belief shapes every aspect of our work as women of color: it disturbs our physical movements through spaces, while it also burdens us with responsibility for institutional labor regarding issues of race, diversity, and inclusion. That is, we are asked to lead the task forces on "diversity issues," speak to our boards about "equity and inclusion," and serve as mentors, leaders, liaisons for any and all conversations, plans, and institutional efforts to save face regarding racial inequality. We are then Band-Aids they hope to put on their hemorrhaging racial wounds.

Sara Ahmed has written extensively about the university and academia in the United Kingdom and Australia. Describing what she calls the "stranger experience" in those institutions, what some of us who cannot pass as white go through when we become noticeable to our institutions precisely because our bodies are assumed to not belong in the whiteness of that space.[5] For me, a light-skinned Black Latina from a working-class background, an immigrant with a Latinx accent, and a graduate of a public university in New Jersey, my strangeness has marked me as lacking what my colleagues often refer to as the "pedigree" required to succeed in the elite university (whiteness, wealth, an Ivy League education, a recognizable last name, maleness, and the support of powerful mentors).[6] In their introduction to *Presumed Incompetent II: Race, Class, Power, and Resistance of Women in Academia*, Yolanda Flores Niemann, Gabriella Gutiérrez y Muhs, and Carmen G. González argue that when it comes to diversity and belonging, the university is "the last bastion of elitism and sanctioned racism in the United States."[7] It is a hostile environment "grounded on racism, sexism, homophobia, and classism" where violence—which takes many forms, as the examples I have shared thus far illustrate—against faculty and students of color is naturalized.

My unbelonging to the university shaped my relationship to colleagues, the administration, and the institution to one of tacit, yet mutual, discomfort. That is, my daily encounters with white colleagues at department meetings and other institutional spaces highlighted how whiteness—being or "acting" white, speaking through whiteness, and performing white civility—was clearly a prerequisite to succeeding as a woman of color scholar in the university. This manifested in subtleties like the colors, brands, and style of our clothes and accessories; our hairdos; and the speech tone, diction, mannerisms, and affect used while speaking in public. I remember, for example, one day at the beginning of a faculty meeting, I bumped into a friend who teaches at a different department and whom I had not seen in almost a year. We hugged and verbally expressed our happiness to see each other. A white male professor looked at us in surprise before stating, "I believe this room has never seen such expressions and effusiveness." He was clearly made uncomfortable by our expressions of affection. I am by nature a warm person. I express care to people. The comment took me by surprise, as it made me realize how much of who I am and how I move in the world is unacceptable within these spaces of whiteness. My failure to perform, understand, speak, and be in harmony with whiteness made me, in Ahmed's term, a "stranger" to the institution: an irreconcilable body that both carried and spread discomfort. As Ahmed writes, "A stranger experience can be an experience of becoming noticeable, of not passing through or passing by, of being stopped or being held up."[8] My strangeness fueled my unbelonging.

While "strangers" like myself are sometimes invited to be part of the elite university through neoliberal practices of diversity and inclusion, ultimately, to preserve the harmony of the institution, we are also asked to assimilate via silence or erasure. Over the years, I have been advised by colleagues to "smile more," "be careful not to let people know you're a single parent," "make sure you don't speak Caribbean Spanish with your colleagues," and perhaps "lose a little weight." Over the years I have also seen other women of color attempt to assimilate to whiteness through both their affect and their bodily performance. One Asian American woman scholar told me she spent hours practicing "the hand gestures white women in my department use to explain theory" after someone let her know that her mannerisms were "too distracting."

We are expected to make white people comfortable with our presence, or we risk being expunged. My unwillingness or inability to be in harmony with whiteness—to mute my strangeness in the institution and accept its implicit white supremacy in all aspects of institutional, curricular, and academic life—culminated in my dismissal from Harvard via tenure denial in 2019.

Being expunged by whiteness via tenure denial was one of the most violent and difficult yet edifying experiences of my career. After spending eight years building up Harvard, working for and with my students, exceeding every expectation in my research, teaching, and service, I received a call, the night before Thanks-giving 2019, from the chair of my department. He said, "Lorgia, dear, I have terrible news. I am so sorry, but you have been denied tenure." I thought he was joking. Weeks prior, my chair, who was a supporter of my work and truly believed I deserved tenure, had sent me a champagne bottle emoji following a message that assured me "everything is going spectacularly" in my tenure process. His assurances and those of the deans made the denial even more cruel. But it took a while for the news to sink in; it took even lon-ger to understand the extent of the violence implicit in this news. As a survivor of emotional and sexual violence, I know all too well how draining and complex the process by which we come to terms with the effects of violence is on our bodies and psyche. How long it takes before we finally see that the harm done is not our fault. The guilt and shame we feel is weaponized by our abusers. It takes dis-tance, time, work, and support to really see ourselves as survivors and to appreciate the courage that it takes to survive.

Institutional violence manifests in multiple insidious ways: denial of equal treatment, abuses in labor practices, unequal pay, unfair amounts of labor, microaggressions, and most of all, cruelty. The cruelty of ending my eight years of service with a phone call on the night before a holiday was yet another example of institu-tional violence. But my tenure denial was the most rational finale to what I often describe as a long-term abusive relationship with my employer—one in which I was simultaneously at the receiving end of both violence and adulation.

Over my years as a tenure-track professor at Harvard Univer-sity, I was regaled with awards, fellowships, an endowed chair, and other forms of recognition. Senior colleagues and administrators often called me "a star" and assured me of how much I mattered to the future of the "new and more diverse institution"—to the deferred project of belonging we were building "together" with and through my labor. Many times, these adulations were contradicted by hate and violence that manifested through human interactions with people in the university community as well as through encounters with the institution via its representatives, my colleagues and administrators.

Some of these interactions shook me to my core, like the instance in which I was attacked on campus in 2016 by two men who threw hot coffee at me while yelling, "Build the wall!" Or when a note was tacked on my office door in 2019 with misogynist and racist insults followed by the words "you don't belong here." Or the time in spring 2020 during a live online lecture when "Zoombombers" called for my death—or more specifically, my lynching. That these happened on campus or while I worked is not a small coincidence. That the administration did nothing to protect me from the violence, instead playing the "thoughts and prayers" card, showed the complicity of individuals and institutions in enacting violence. That I spoke against these violent acts, that I complained publicly, made me "ungrateful" in the eyes of the institution and therefore unworthy of its protection.

And yet, my experiences with institutional violence are not unique. In fact, while filling out a police report after the 2019 hate crime of the note placed on my office door, the officer in charge of the investigation, a Black man, told me that these instances are common at Harvard. He said, "They don't want to see us [POC] shine. They want you quiet. Your voice is a threat to the status quo." While I was taken aback by the sincerity of the officer, I wasn't surprised to hear that racial violence is common on Harvard campus. Two other professors, both women of color, told me in confidence that they, too, had been receiving notes and aggressive phone calls, that they had been called racial and misogynist slurs. When I asked them to come forward with me, they declined, citing fear of repercussion from the administration. One of them said to me, "If I speak out against this, all I gain is more attention to myself as a complainer.

You got to take this with your head down, at least until tenure. It is an unwinnable fight."

It has taken me almost two years to recognize the violence of working in academia and that led to my tenure denial. I am still working through it. From past experiences, I know the pain will always be there to some extent. But now I can name it. Institutional violence is real, I know because my body knew. My body remembers the pain. I still shake when I see a note left under my door, or when I receive a letter from someone I don't know. I still feel unsafe walking to a garage after a public lecture. I am watchful. I no longer walk with headphones listening to Nina Simone, as I used to. I need all my senses alert, just in case someone from around a corner decides to throw hot coffee at me and call me a slur. I suspect—expect—the worst, and my body reacts accordingly, ready to flee and search for survival.

While these examples are extreme, they were not the only instances of violence I experienced. Others, like the microaggressions of colleagues who asked me to "smile more" or not be so "angry" or to be careful not to upset the way things are became part of my daily reality, minor obstacles. I grew used to confronting them by kindly returning the discomfort, by pointing out the multiple ways their discomfort with my person, my scholarship, and my words was a sign of their white privilege. When the news of my tenure denial came, however, all those encounters, big and small, fell together like pieces of a puzzle. Suddenly everything made sense. In the weeks that followed the news, I took out seven years' worth of journals and began to reread my story, becoming reacquainted with the genealogy of my "strangeness."

One of the most tangible ways I was made a stranger on campus was through the constant racial profiling I was subjected to by campus police, security, and staff. During my first semester at Harvard, for example, entering the building where my office was located, I was reminded of how my minoritized body does not belong in elite university spaces. Unlike colleges in other parts of the United States where buildings are highly secured, Harvard was fairly open and unpoliced during working hours. While security desks in buildings were common, I never observed anyone else being detained by security personnel. Yet, this happened to me daily for several weeks. The white security guard seated at the front desk of the Barker Center, where my office was located, approached me with an aggressive tone one day as I entered, saying that this was not a public building. Stunned, I said that I did know that and kept walking, only to be stopped again and asked to present my ID. These encounters continued for weeks until I reported it to my department chair, who intervened on my behalf. No apologies were ever offered by the administration or staff.

In 2016, I hosted a visiting scholar from Italy who is a Black woman. As her host, I wanted to give her a short tour of the library between her talks and class visits. As we entered the foyer of the main library (after I checked us in at the help desk and obtained permission to bring in a guest), the clerk at the front desk, a white woman, approached us aggressively, asking if we thought we could just sneak in without permission, I was so shocked and embarrassed I didn't respond. To this day, my visitor, who has now become a close friend, remembers the incident as her "crash course on American racism." Years later, I bumped into the same library clerk at the dissertation defense of one of my students. She had apparently taken a language course for which he had been the teaching assistant and was thus invited to the event. At the reception she approached me with the exoticizing curiosity I had become accustomed to experiencing when white colleagues figured out that I was a professor. I would typically get questions like, "Where are you from?" When I replied that I am from Trenton, New Jersey, the response was generally something like, "Fascinating." The idea of a Black Latina professor with a working-class background in an elite university was "fascinating"—another commodity to sell in the project of diversity and inclusion. The clerk was "fascinated" by me now that she knew I was a professor. She wanted to chat about literature, learn about my research, see if she could audit my class. I cut her off by asking if she remembered me, adding that we indeed had met. She looked at me for a minute, then said, I looked familiar but she could not place me. She thought perhaps she had attended one of my lectures. After explaining to her how we had met, I told her that while she barely recognized me, I could never forget her face because racism always haunts those who experience it. She apologized and quickly moved away from me. Despite her embarrassment, she continued to work the room, sipping wine and finding ways to butter up other professors. Her immense privilege allowed her to remain in a space that was mine (it was my department, my student, an event I had organized), despite the discomfort she caused me. Unlike her, I could not stay. I left the gathering early—another practice I have become accustomed to in my life as The One.

While these examples of daily violent encounters with policing and racializing exclusion were traumatizing to say the least, by far the most egregious example of my experiences of being policed took place in class. On a rare sunny February day in 2015, I decided to take my mostly Black and brown students to the main quad for an outdoor class. We were in the middle of conducting class when the campus police interrupted, demanding IDs and letting us know we were not allowed to be there. They were responding to a call from a concerned staff member, they said, about disturbances on the yard. We were reading poetry. At the time I didn't realize this experience would become the norm for me and, sadly, for my students. Every time I attempted to host my class outside, the police would interrupt, questioning my right and my students' right to be on campus. They did this even when I took preventative steps by planning and securing permission to hold class outside (something my white colleagues did not have to do). We continued to be interrupted by the police through my last semester teaching at Harvard. No measures I took ever prevented it. The fact is, we did not meet their expectations of belonging. We were strangers who threatened the white supremacy of the space, making some white members of the institution uncomfortable. And white discomfort is not allowed within the colonizing project of the university—that is, the project by which the university creates hierarchies of people, knowledge, and spaces based on race. This process of exclusion—the colonizing project—is framed around narratives aimed at sustaining the dominant structures of power while also securing the complicity of students and faculty through investment in ideas of unity, progress, and diversity that are based on whiteness.

Being a stranger on campus is a violent experience grounded in the colonial order that engendered and sustains white supremacy. When I talk about the elite university as a colonial and colonizing space, people are sometimes shocked. We are so intent on believing that academia is a benevolent institution that we tend to forget that many of our elite university buildings were physically built by enslaved people on stolen land so that white men would be able to train the next generation of those who belong: white men. While Black, Indigenous, Latinx, and other minoritized students have been part of higher education for centuries, they have always been a minority. They are presumed to be a "selection," always imagined as exceptions.

The presence of faculty of color, particularly women, in the university has been even rarer. It was only in 1976 that Harvard hired a Black woman lecturer for the first time. Eileen Jackson Southern, a musicologist, was eventually tenured at Harvard, becoming the chair of what was then called the Department of Afro-American Studies.

In 1988, Yale tenured its first Black woman professor, Sylvia Ardyn Boone, a scholar of African art. Niara Sudarkasa was appointed at the University of Michigan in 1969 in the Department of Anthropology, earning tenure in the mid-1970s, and Berkeley tenured Barbara Christian in 1978. That the history of Black women faculty is this recent, and that the abovementioned women continued to be the only full professors in their departments and many times in the entire institution for over a decade, shows how slow the university is at enacting its project of "diversity and inclusion," even when said project is mandated by legislation. The short history of Black and women of color faculty in the ranks of the university is no anomaly. Rather, it is the backbone of the continuous project of diversity that sustains the logic and praxis of The One.

As of 2021, the Department of Romance Languages and Literatures at Harvard University has never tenured a Black professor. While Harvard has tenured several Black faculty over the last two decades, most of them are in the same department: African and African American Studies (AAAS). Non-US Black, Black scholars outside of the AAAS field, and in particular, scholars of ethnic studies who are not white, continue to face challenges in hiring, promotion, and tenure processes at Harvard. The same is true across the country in most universities, particularly so in elite and Ivy League institutions that refuse to recognize ethnic studies as a legitimate field of knowledge production and teaching.[9] While ethnic studies has indeed existed for more than half a century, many colleges and universities are resistant to the creation of departments that would institutionalize what in their view are spaces for "activism" rather than the legitimate fields of inquiry they are.[10] Paired with the fact that ethnic studies is concerned with the lives, works, and histories of minoritized, colonized people and that since its inception the field has emerged as a site of contestation against the colonizing structures of academia, universities, particularly elite schools, are never happy to institutionalize ethnic studies and give it the power and legitimacy it deserves. For example, out of the top twenty elite universities in the United States, only UC Berkeley, a public institution and one of the sites of the original Third World Liberation Front strikes in 1968–1969, has a department of ethnic studies. While some progress has been gained in the last decade due to student activism and national pressure from scholars in the field, all the Ivy League and most elite schools continue to deny students' petitions to create departments dedicated to the studies of Latinx, Asian, Native, and Black Americans.[11]

The stories I share throughout this book lay out a historical linearity that outlines my own path as a Black Latina on the tenure track in an elite institution. They also outline—in rather simple if violent terms—the ontology of The One. The project of limiting racial and ethnic diversity and representation to The One exists in harmony with that of "diversity and inclusion." It is its offspring. Diversity and inclusion stems from the need to comply with the equal opportunity employment objectives implemented in the Civil Rights Act of 1964. Colleges and universities have the obligation to implement affirmative action policies aimed at correcting the exclusion and disenfranchisement of nonwhite students as well as white women students who had been denied access to equal education since the existence of universities in the United States. While many public universities used affirmative action as an opportunity to make campuses more diverse, elite schools continued to exclude students of color based on notions of merit that did not consider economic inequality. As such, only a handful of students of color were admitted, and elite campuses continued to be mostly white until the demographic shifts of the twenty-first century forced a reckoning that has led to a significant increase in admission of students of color, most of them first-generation college students. While the admission of students of color to elite institutions continues to grow, hiring practices for faculty have not changed to match the demographics of the student body. There continues to be a marginal number of faculty of color across colleges and universities in the United States.[12] It is thus not surprising that for a few years I was the only Latina on the tenure track in the entire faculty of arts and sciences.

The existence of The One allows the university to maintain the status quo, to continue to operate in harmony with whiteness while saving face publicly. The One is the perfect representation of the deferred project of inclusion, a project we know is not about justice or equity. To have The One allows institutions to say, "See? We are not racists. See? We are moving forward. We have started creating an inclusive institution." Being The One is being forced into complicity with your own exclusion and unbelonging and with your own strangeness. To be The One means behaving, obeying the rules of whiteness, maintaining the status quo, and above all, being grateful. That gratitude is demonstrated through silence and complicity. The One must never complain. We must be understanding and let microaggressions pass. When I complained about the violence I was experiencing as The One in my daily life on campus, I was offered explanations about how whatever transpired was no one's fault, that there were no "ill intentions." My discomfort and the violence I suffered were all part of the "misunderstanding" that my "strangeness," to borrow from Ahmed once again, provoked. The message was clear: People like you do not belong here. You are the exception. You are The One, and being The One comes at a cost. To be The One you must be willing to accept your own discomfort and quietly conform to whiteness. You must be willing to comply to make white people comfortable.

Over the years, I have accumulated hundreds of stories about the everyday violence of being The One and the multiple ways the university reinforces and maintains a tacit quota system to avoid rebellion. As I found myself the resident woman of color in multiple departments and committees, it stopped being surprising and I came to expect it. And while it was exhausting and exploitative to play this role, I also came to understand that serving as the resident woman of color was the only way to ensure there would be more of us. On hiring and admissions committees, I raised my voice to remind everyone that, per their own decision, my role in *their* project of diversity and inclusion was to remind them to be inclusive and diverse. Sometimes it worked. In 2015, I was asked to serve on a hiring committee for a position that did not relate directly to my field. I had become accustomed to these requests. It was my fourth such role on a committee. I understood I was being asked, once more, to serve as The One. At the beginning of our meeting, I made it clear that I would participate in the committee under two conditions: (1) we would make every effort to hire a woman of color, and (2) we would require a mentoring statement to weed out faculty who were unwilling to or uninterested in supporting students—particularly first-generation and minoritized students. While some of the members of the committee were not thrilled about my requests, I made it clear that my service was conditional. I returned my discomfort at being made The One by explicitly letting them know that I understood my role, and I refused to play by their rules. I would not allow them to pretend my racialized body did not exist while they used it to exemplify their "diversity." My conditional labor yielded multiple hires of tenure-track faculty, lecturers, and postdoctoral fellows of color. Sometimes it even led to wonderful collaborations with and allyship against institutional practices of the colonizing university in ways that reflect the call that Robin D. G. Kelley made in his 2016 essay "Black Study, Black Struggle." To not ask the university to "love us back," to not demand the university—a neoliberal, colonizing, racializing institution—provide that which is against its own nature, but rather to take its resources and structures and repurpose them to create freedom spaces, freedom schools, and liberation moments within and through its violent exclusion. Making our labor conditional—returning the discomfort, flipping the project of diversity and inclusion even if only briefly—is an act of freedom-making that contradicts the logic of The One.[13]

Some of the pervasive effects of being The One are common knowledge among faculty of color, particularly women faculty of color: we are pressured to serve on committees, undervalued, underpaid, untenured, and struggling to be promoted. One effect—the most pervasive, in my opinion—is hardly spoken about, however: the way the logic of "there can be only one of us" undermines our efforts to build community, create solidarity, and support each other through the tumultuous tenure track. This reality is, of course, less common in departments and universities with a critical mass of faculty of color working in ethnic studies fields. But for those of us working in institutions that are majority white, working in ethnic studies or smaller interdisciplinary fields, and struggling to make our work visible while our white colleagues dismiss it as unimportant navel-gazing or too narrow, this crude reality shapes our relationships with one another—at times, even across campuses and even when we don't know each other.

In spring 2013, shortly after being offered a tenure-track position at Harvard University and while still working at the University of Georgia, I attended a Latinx literature conference at John Jay College of Criminal Justice in New York City. After my presentation, I was bombarded with a series of aggressive questions from one of the attendees, a person of color. While I found their tone and line of questioning puzzling, nothing had prepared me for what happened at the end of the panel presentation. This person came up to me and said that they had been a finalist for the position I had held for three years at the University of Georgia. They were upset because the position was offered to me instead of them, and I was now leaving.

They said to me that it was not fair that I had *another* tenure-track offer while they didn't. I was stunned by the bitterness with which I was being interpellated, but mostly I was saddened that at a conference about Latinx literature, someone else in my field—another person of color who was suffering in the academy due to the neoliberal practices of the elite university—saw *me* as their enemy rather than engage in a critical examination of the systemic exclusion of ethnic studies fields that has left many of us competing for only a handful of positions. According to this person, it was my fault they did not get their desired job.

I had graduated from the University of Michigan with a PhD right after the 2008 market crash. Upon completing my degree requirements, and while five months pregnant, I found myself in an academic job market with only four jobs in Latinx studies. Many of us recent graduates were at risk of unemployment. Given my working-class and immigrant background, I had begun to consider alternative options, looking at jobs outside of academia. Right when I was about to give up, an out-of-cycle position at the University of Georgia was announced, and my dissertation adviser Larry Lafountain-Stokes encouraged me to apply. I accepted my first tenure-track position at the University of Georgia in 2010.

Moving to Georgia posed many personal challenges for me, as I left behind my network and family and moved far away with a newborn baby. The years in Georgia, though, proved to be the most formative of my career, and I will be forever grateful for that experience. In 2013, after dealing with attacks from white supremacist groups due to my activism in support of the undocumented community, I went back on the job market to move closer to my family and put some distance between myself and the racism and violence I was experiencing in Georgia. The decision was heart-wrenching, and the transition was hard. I was leaving behind a community I had helped build and work that was sustaining me in multiple ways.

I had not yet made the physical move to Massachusetts at the time of the conference in New York, nor had I publicly announced my acceptance of the Harvard position. In that context, the accost by the attendee not only shocked me; it shook me.

Years later, after my book *The Borders of Dominicanidad* was published, a fellow Latina scholar in the field made a similar remark about me to a group of Latinx scholars at a major conference. Two of my close friends were present. She was wounded that my book "had taken all the attention," making it impossible for people to notice *her* book, which came out two years or so after mine. According to her, my success limited hers. Apparently, there could be only one book in our field—or at least that was the message she had received from her colleagues and advisers. She rejoiced at the fact that I did not get tenure at Harvard because this meant I would finally get out of her way. One of my friends confronted her in a kind yet assertive way, asking her to see the harm that her words and ill wishes for a fellow Latina scholar reflected not only on her but on all of us. But the scholar could not hear my friend. Her mind was made up, and she thought of me as her enemy and the cause of her inability to obtain the imaginary grand prize of being The One.

In both these cases, my fellow scholars participated in the logic of The One, placing blame on my person and scholarship rather than on the institutions that create and sustain this toxic logic. As in some violent video game, there could be only one winner once all the competition was eliminated; thus I—along with any other "competition"—would need to be eliminated for them to succeed. The logic of The One is inherently violent. Believing ourselves to be The (Deserving) One can be, as in the examples of these two scholars, paralyzing, isolating, and incredibly damaging. While both these scholars have successful careers (one of them obtained tenure at an elite institution), their glaring complicity with the university colonizing project hindered their ability to create freedom spaces for themselves and their students, for their energy was focused on becoming The (Only) One. This pervasive logic threatens the very essence of who we are and have been as a community, how we survive in the face of white supremacy, and how we grow and thrive as women of color scholars.

The project of the corporate white supremacist colonizing university endorses minoritized representation but through a model of "diversity and inclusion" that's grounded in white domination. Faculty of color in predominantly white institutions, as sociologist Ramona Hernández reminds us, are a disposable labor force who serve and support the growing population of first-generation students of color but who are not invited into the fabric of the institution as tenured faculty, deans, or administrators in a collective way that would ensure true representation and the possibility of systemic change.[14] For example, according to a 2019 report from the National Center for Education Statistics, 6 percent of assistant professors nationwide are Latinas. At the full professor rank, we are only 3 percent. Meanwhile, white men hold 34 percent of assistant professor positions and 54 percent of full professor positions nationwide.[15] Notably, these numbers do not account for race within the Latinx community. We would be hard pressed to find a dozen Black Latinas at the full professor level in the humanities, for example, in the entire United States. By contrast, Latinx, and particularly Latinas, compose 32 percent of the untenured, adjunct, and temporary workforce in our colleges and universities across the United States.[16] These numbers show that there is not truly a "diversity" problem but rather a problem of power. "Diverse" faculty—part-time lecturers and adjuncts—are brought in to teach most courses, advise students, and provide staff support. However, when it comes to those on the tenure track (assistant, associate, and full professors), our numbers are limited, and our capacity to participate in decision-making is thwarted by the persistent logic of The One. This ensures that the project of representational diversity and inclusion remains intact (by way of having One of us to demonstrate "diversity") while simultaneously denying us the possibility of rebellion against systematic racism in the institution. Effective rebellion requires numbers. Instead, the few of us who do rebel become targets of retaliation, exposing ourselves to institutional violence and risking our careers.

Rebelling as "The One" Is Career Suicide

During my years as a tenure-track professor of Latinx studies, I rebelled, loudly and forcefully, against the logic of The One and the systematic ways the university ensured that the fields of Latinx and ethnic studies remained marginal despite overwhelming student interest and demands for institutional support. At times my rebellion seemed impactful, as I witnessed small victories, such as the creation of a minor in ethnic studies for undergraduate students, a graduate certificate program in Latinx Studies for doctoral students, the growth of the number of doctoral students of color in my program, the increase in a university dialogue about the urgency of creating an ethnic studies program, and the hiring of colleagues of color. Parallel to these small victories were the immensely painful moments of aggression that ranged from off-handed comments from senior faculty and direct threats against my career to the defacing of my office door with racial slurs and my tenure denial. Still, as I look back over this abusive eight-year relationship with my employer, those small victories fill me with hope for what is possible if we keep growing and rebelling, not as individuals, but as a community.

In her numerous writings about teaching and love, bell hooks insisted on community-building as salvation. She writes, "*Beloved community* is formed not by the eradication of difference but by its affirmation, by each of us claiming the identities and cultural legacies that shape who we are and how we live in the world."[17] Particularly for those of us who identify as BIPOC (Black, Indigenous, and people of color) or women of color working within anticolonial frameworks, knowledge-making, community, and the experience of cocreating are essential. They are the only ways to critically rebel against the colonial racial-capitalist regime that pits us against each other through the narrative of exceptionalism. Community contra*dicts* the pervasive logic of The One.[18]

Building community, though, is almost antithetical to academia. Grounded in a model of individual success that rewards white men and the knowledge they have created for centuries, academia promotes competitiveness, exceptionalism, and ownership of history and knowledge-making. We are primed to believe we "find" history in an archive and therefore own it. We come up with ideas about major processes in society—from colonialism to historical legacies of oppression—and imagine no one else could possibly share similar thoughts, even when these are based on human experiences we share. We hold our critical thoughts and our important insights hostage until graced with coveted peer-reviewed publications that can forever grant us the seal of ownership. In the humanities, only single-authored books count toward tenure, coteaching is discouraged, and group projects, while laudable, are another form of unrewarded labor. And yet, while this logic of suspicion and individual ownership of knowledge dominates every aspect of academia, from student assignments to tenure decisions, we know that how we truly grow as scholars and learners is through collective exchange, generosity, and kindness. It is through engaging with one another and through difference—through theorizing from our own flesh, as Latina feminist writer Cherríe Moraga invites us to do—that we become better scholars, better teachers, and wiser human beings.

Students protesting the denial of tenure of García Peña on Harvard campus

Through the ups and downs of my academic career, I have thought long and hard about the meaning of being The One and the urgent, unequivocal need to strengthen and support our communities as women of color in academia in the face of white supremacy. Poet and Black feminist scholar Camara Brown reminds us that care, kinship, and friendship have been the building blocks of Black and women of color feminism.[19] It is from profound love and care for each other and a desire for solidarity that Moraga's foundational women of color feminist anthology *This Bridge Called My Back* came to be. That love is a legacy that comes from the life experiences of being in and living with these bodies and recognizing that to survive systemic oppression, racial capitalism, and white supremacy, mutual care is as important as self-care.

In the Dominican Republic, where I was born, women in working and farming communities share the load of everyday life, including child-rearing, cooking, and farming. In the *rayano* (borderland) community of Jimaní, for example, women nurse each other's babies (a practice unthinkable in the Global North), making the responsibilities—and bodies—of motherhood communal. I call this understanding of the world as shared "*rayano* consciousness."[20] *Rayano* consciousness also manifests tacitly in feminist praxis such as the practice of community caring for a woman after childbirth, the kitchen-table feminism in which women plot together to take down aggressors such as molesters and abusive husbands, and the political space of the hair salon, where, as sociologist Ginetta Candelario teaches us, immigrant women in the diaspora gain access to everything from legal representation to childcare.[21] Women of color have been taking care of one another for centuries. It is through our communal care that we have managed to survive the atrocities of slavery, colonialism, capitalism, and migration. It is through our reliance on one another that our histories—despite being erased and silenced from official archives—continue to emerge and be re-membered to sustain us.

So, how do we remember to care for each other *together* in academia? How do we hold ourselves and others in the face of an individualistic racial-capital regime that insists we remain isolated from one another—that we "eliminate the competition" to succeed through the logic of exceptionalism?

First, we need to recognize and understand that our legacy, who we are and how we have come to occupy the space we do in academia—and on this earth—has been the result of collective rebellion. Robin D. G. Kelley reminds us that "resistance is our heritage" and our healing.[22] For someone like myself—a migrant, a Black Latina, the daughter of working people—to be able to write, think, and speak from this place of immense privilege means many who came before me rebelled, loudly and persistently, to create this space I now hold. They fought against my oppressors. Then made their backs bridges so I could cross. Others extended a hand so I would not fall. Still others cheered me on as I got tired, and some took over when I did get tired, holding me and that space until I was ready to continue. None of us got here on our own. Others, people we know and people we do not know, rebelled to create space, to make room, so we would fit. The narrative that we arrived on our own, by pulling up our bootstraps, is a toxic fiction.

Second, we must collectively force the universities to see the violence they perpetuate on our persons, our bodies, our psyches, and our scholarship. The testimonies shared in the #BlackIn-TheIvory archive—a social media project through which people share their experiences of violence and oppression as Black scholars in the US university and in the two volumes of the *Presumed Incompetent* anthology—make visible our collective pain. The repetition and recognition I experienced reading these testimonies is disheartening. How many of these stories were my own! How many times had I had many of these same experiences? This violence is so much a part of our collective experience. And yet, it keeps happening. These experiences will be the rites of passage for the next generation of young BIPOC scholars. Unless we stop it. Unless we rebel in community to, as Kelley writes, "alter our circumstances; contain, escape, or possibly eviscerate the *source* of trauma; recover our bodies; reclaim and redeem our dead; and make ourselves whole."[23] Community rebellion is our antidote to the violence of being The One.

The project of "diversity and inclusion" that many of us are forced to represent does not lead to freedom or justice. Rather, as Chicana feminist writer Gloria Anzaldúa and, more recently, Sara Ahmed have argued, it yields a language of comfort that allows white supremacy to name us in the very process of creating our exclusion. Following Anzaldúa, Ahmed argues, "If the zone of diversity is one of comfort, then diversity might provide a cushion, both softening the edge of critique and allowing institutions to be reinhabited as softer spaces."[24] Take, for example, the relatively recent practice of reading land acknowledgments prior to any university event in North America. Faculty and administrators perform the reading of a land acknowledgment in an almost automatic way, without contemplating the implications that the university sits on stolen land built by enslaved labor to support and justify the project of colonizing exclusion. In this acknowledgment of colonization, there are typically no plans for working toward ending systematic exclusion or abolishing dispossession, violence, and colonizing logic from the institution that perpetuates inequality. What does it mean to say "we acknowledge that we are sitting on stolen land" if that acknowledgment is not followed by institutional practices aimed at redressing some of the pain it continues to inflict upon the descendants of dispossessed, enslaved, and colonized peoples? That many times land acknowledgments are read in universities that do not have Native American and Indigenous studies programs further exemplifies Anzaldúa's argument that the language of diversity and inclusion only repeats the violence of exclusion.[25] Native dispossession continues in the present even as universities acknowledge it in the past; exclusion is perpetuated in the very act of claiming "diversity and inclusion."

Third, we must insist—by any means necessary—on recognition for the totality of our labor: the hours spent supporting the students of color the university ignores; the months of service on committees; the emotional and mental labor required of us to exist as The One; the love and care that we put into our teaching, advising, and mentoring; and the significance of our public-facing work. That "invisible" labor needs to become visible, evaluated, rewarded, valued, and compensated as much as our research. It needs to count toward tenure and promotion. That "other" labor should also become required of all faculty, not just The One. We need to organize collectively to withhold our labor—our participation in perpetuating the violence and exclusion of the elite university— through boycotts that shed light on unfair institutional practices.

In 2020, the University of Mississippi fired Garrett Felber, a brilliant scholar of Black history and a dedicated activist in the fight against mass incarceration. Felber was fired for allegedly "failing to sufficiently communicate with his department chair."[26] In reality, he was dismissed because he took a stand against the university's practice of accepting donations from donors who profit from the prison-industrial system. After his dismissal, scholars from across the United States pledged to boycott Ole Miss, withdrawing our labor until the university agreed to reinstate him. The boycott sent a strong message to the university—and to academia as a whole— while challenging the increasingly common practices of retaliation against outspoken professors that in the last decade have left many brilliant scholars jobless. In the end, the university settled a lawsuit with Felber, who has continued writing and researching in freedom. The boycott in support of Felber is one example of how we can effectively respond as a community in the face of injustice by leveraging our labor and reminding institutions that without our work, they cannot exist.

Finally, we must rebel—collectively, loudly, tirelessly—against the toxic logic of The One that threatens our careers and our lives. Rebelling is a communal process. It requires all of us to recognize, as the editors of *Presumed Incompetent II* urge us to do, that academia is hurting women of color and we must therefore fight back: "We realize that the best antidote for this disease of death by academia is to be communal and transparent about the hostile contexts experienced by too many of our colleagues."[27] We must thus rebel together, shattering silences, responding loudly to return the discomfort we are made to feel as we exist as strangers within the university, leveraging our labor within their project of "diversity and inclusion," withholding our labor when our work is not valued or compensated, refusing to accept positions as The One (and naming our refusal publicly), letting our students know what it means to be The One when we find ourselves there, and refusing to stay silent. But most importantly, we must rebel by creating communities of freedom within and outside the institution, by reaching out to others and forming concrete plans to sustain our work and our lives. These can take the form of writing collectives, of freedom schools, of co-ops of care where political, social, and human actions can be articulated and carried to support one another. I have helped build such spaces, and they have saved me. In these communities we can hold each other, give each other the benefit of the doubt, embrace a space of compassion. We can offer a hand to pull us through, a back to help us cross, and a shoulder where we can safely rest our heads for a brief moment until we can lift them up again and keep on.

Community is the most effective form of rebellion.

2.

READING LIST
Complicity with Whiteness Will Not Save You

When I was a young girl, I loved sitting on the sofa with my dad, watching action movies—the kind with a smart heist and a thief getting away with robbing a bank or stealing jewelry from the superrich. I remember feeling a sort of moral guilt at my desire to see the robber get away with the crime. Wasn't stealing bad? Shouldn't I be siding with the cops? One time, I must have been seven or eight years old, I asked my dad if we were becoming accomplices to the crime by watching these movies and cheering for the "bad guys." He paused, smiled, and looked at me for a long time before answering something beautiful and incredibly profound that through the faulty and cloudy memory of my early childhood (and after multiple attempts at reconstructing the scene with my dad over the years), I've chosen to memorialize as follows: Complicity means you are working with or benefiting from some form of wrongdoing. We have not robbed the bank, nor have we gotten any of the money, have we? This is all for pretend. But there is a good lesson here, my daughter. Always look out for the accomplices in any bad situation, people who would cause you harm just to get ahead, to get a cut of the loot. They are everywhere, and sometimes, many times, they pretend to be your friend. On the other hand, make sure you find your own accomplices, the people who would support you and help overcome the difficult things in life—that, too, is necessary for survival in this world.

While I did not fully comprehend my father's advice at the time and while I cannot remember verbatim everything he said, I never forgot the meaning his words carried; nor did I forget the sense of uneasiness they provoked in me. Years later, that uneasiness continues to haunt me as I understand how the complicity of my colleagues sustains the colonizing structures of the university that produce the logic of The One and exclude faculty of color from belonging.

What does it mean to be an accomplice to the university's colonizing project of exclusion and unbelonging? And more importantly, how do we protect ourselves from the harm that such complicity can inflict on our lives and careers as women of color scholars? How do we find accomplices with whom to fight back?

When we contemplate complicity, we tend to think about active participation in a process—the robbers who populated my dad's eighties heist movies. But the complicity that I experienced in my own exclusion and estrangement from the university—the complicity that makes it possible for the university to continue to exist through and in harmony with white supremacy—is not always active. Rather, it is shaped by the passive and tacit participation of faculty and administrators—particularly, though not only, white senior faculty—who benefit from the inequality these structures support. The biggest challenge in fighting against the colonizing structures of the university is precisely its accomplices. Accomplices occupy many spaces and play many roles in the colonizing project. They help sustain the status quo through which the university professes a commitment to diversity and inclusion while continuing to exclude our knowledges, people, and histories through ignorance, silence, greed, and fear. The biggest challenge to those of us leading the fight to decolonize the university is that its accomplices are many, and they are often unwilling to see their own complicity.[1]

Let's consider tenure again, this time as a site of complicity. Faculty of color, particularly Black and Latina women, make up less than 2 percent of tenured full professors in the United States.[2] This is not for lack of trying. From the moment we arrive at graduate school to the final stages of our promotion, the odds are stacked against us. Getting tenure and being promoted as a woman of color are rare and difficult occurrences. The fact that losing tenure means you must leave the university, that you are fired, makes it a violent and traumatizing process, as Grace Park explains in her powerful essay "My Tenure Denial":

> A tenure denial is made to seem as if it is the sole respon-
> sibility of the person denied tenure, but it is also evidence
> of a department's and institution's collective failure to ade-
> quately mentor, integrate, and help their junior colleague
> navigate the hidden rules, culture, and politics of their spe-
> cific institution. It is ultimately a shared responsibility, but
> because the process is not transparent, systemic patterns
> of bias may never be addressed, thereby perpetuating the
> myth of meritocracy in academia and rendering the chal-
> lenges Women of Color face in the tenure process invisible.[3]

The structures of tenure and promotion at colleges and universities systematically put faculty of color at a disadvantage, hindering our advancement and jeopardizing our freedom of speech. Ironically, the same faculty who are in most need of the protections afforded by tenure—Black, brown, Indigenous, and Asian faculty working in nontraditional fields or who are politically involved in liberation struggles—are the ones for whom tenure has become a task as difficult as climbing Mount Everest. There are multiple reasons for this.

First, as the examples shared in chapter 1 illustrate, many faculty members of color are made to pay what Joann Trejo calls the "minority tax," in which faculty of color are burdened with extra responsibilities to help the university achieve its diversity and inclusion goals. For Trejo, the "minority tax" made it so not only was she overburdened with responsibility and strapped for time to conduct her research but she also worried that her colleagues in the sciences would not take her work seriously and "would question my credibility and commitment to science."[4]

The minority tax, paired with lack of mentorship and institutional support, often leads to unfair labor practices, most notably the burden of conducting research in our spare time—almost as an afterthought—while being evaluated for tenure solely or mostly on the quantity and quality of said research. This incredibly unfair system mimics the colonizing structures of racial capitalism in which Black, brown, Indigenous, and Asian workers perform most of what we now call *essential labor*: work that is critical for the survival and sustenance of our society but that is poorly compensated, dangerous to the people performing it, and viewed by society as remedial. In the process, BIPOC essential workers are exposed to harm and barely make enough money to sustain themselves. During the COVID-19 pandemic, we have normalized the performative public praise of "essential workers" (signs on our windows and doors, in speeches, and so on), yet we do very little to make their lives more livable: minimum wage has not been raised in most states for almost a decade, union and workers' protections are nonexistent for most essential workers, and the communities from which these workers come have been the last to receive access to COVID testing and vaccines. In addition, many essential workers are also undocumented migrants who are at risk of deportation. We do very little to acknowledge their essential labor—in work such as farming, grocery delivery, and elder care—and speak only of their "sacrifice," as if said sacrifice was indeed a choice rather than the result of racial capitalism and inequality. We speak of them as a mass, never unpacking the nuances of who they are: migrants and minoritized people of color whom our capitalist system exploit for the comfort of the rest of us. While the challenges faced by faculty of color are in no way on par with those of essential workers, they stem from the same racial-capitalist system. That is, universities reproduce inequality among their faculty and students through exclusionary acts that both promote "diversity and inclusion" and at the same time ensure that the people who make the university diverse experience violence, exclusion, and unbelonging.

That is the case of an assistant professor of Latinx studies at a state university in New England whom I will call Maria, to protect her privacy. A brown woman from the West Coast, she was the only Latina serving in a humanities department at her institution. Maria reached out to me after learning about my tenure denial in the news, and we met over Zoom in early 2020. In one of the multiple conversations we had that year, Maria explained to me how the complicity of her white senior colleagues with the exploitative system shaped her experience in academia, eventually leading to the denial of her tenure and her eventual departure from academia:

> I was completely unprepared for what the tenure track would entail. I did not realize it would be six jobs in one and that I would have twenty different bosses. Essentially all my senior colleagues asked me to do things, to join things, to help with things, and I never felt I could say no. The few times I tried to say no, I was reminded of my place, of my position as untenured. I worked eighty hours a week on class preparation and service. There was simply no time for anything else. When my third-year review came, I had little to show by way of my own writing. No one was interested in seeing the hundreds of hours of service I had been

made to complete. Needless to say, I did not fare well in the review. It was clear I was not going to make it, but I kept trying. I doubled down on my research, made myself sick from lack of sleep. Published, but it was not enough. Three years later, I was denied tenure at the department level. I left the academy. I am still heartbroken about it.[5]

As she recalled her experience many years later over our Zoom coffee date, her eyes teared up. The trauma was still visible in her body. Not one single colleague had stood with or for Maria. Instead, they reaped the benefits of her exploitation by the university, as they were relieved from the essential labor she performed. Her courses, the largest in the department, attracted many Black and brown first-generation students, making the department more "diverse," and therefore successful in the eyes of the administration.[6] For Maria, this meant she had more papers to grade, more students to serve, and longer office hours. For her colleagues, it meant they were now part of a lively, successful department without having to put in the inhumane number of labor hours Maria was dedicating to her teaching and service. The fact that enrollment influences how the administration allocates resources also meant Maria's colleagues, particularly her senior colleagues, benefited from institutional support, funding, and other resources because of *her* labor. Yet Maria was never recognized for her contributions. She recalls, "I would sit in the faculty meetings as my chair, a white man, would boast with pride at the number of new majors and at our growth in diversity—not once acknowledging my labor. These were my students! I brought these kids to the department. I mentored them. They were there because of me. My colleagues took my work and made it theirs, all the while disappearing me."[7]

Disappearing and appropriating our labor is all too familiar to many women of color in academia. For me the most tangible example of being disappeared came in the form of a memo sent by the dean of arts and sciences to the faculty and students on December 9, 2019.[8] The memo was a response to student demands for ethnic studies in the wake of my tenure denial. In the memo she listed the "incredible advances" the university had made in the field of ethnic studies and her personal efforts in supporting the field. These advances included the creation of a minor, a graduate certificate in Latinx studies, and a postdoctoral program. All these accomplishments were initiatives I had advanced; they were all the fruit of my labor, yet as the dean mentioned *her* commitment and the university accomplishments, she did not credit me. My work became *their* work while I was erased from the labor I had performed for nearly a decade.

Jane, a Black woman professor of Caribbean studies at an elite New England college, also experienced being disappeared as her labor was co-opted by her department and senior (white) colleagues. She had developed a curriculum, a lecture series, and a mentoring program, which helped the department flourish.[9] Yet not only was she not rewarded for her labor but she was also displaced, and her role was suddenly erased in all departmental written documentation. Proactively she went to see her dean to enlist support. She recalls, "I was furious. I wanted recognition, yes, but most of all, I wanted it to stop."[10] In her meeting, the dean, who is a Black man, nodded and sympathized but did not offer any solutions. She remembers feeling physically ill as she explained to him the injustices she experienced in her department, only to have him nod and admit this was simply the way things are. Unlike Maria, who left academia, Jane fought hard and long for recognition, eventually obtaining tenure at a public university in the Midwest. Yet her fight—and more importantly, "the complicity of my colleagues with the system that nearly killed me"—came at a high cost to her physical and mental health. She developed a chronic illness, depression, and anxiety and exhibited PTSD symptoms for nearly a decade.[11]

The minority tax and erasure of our labor are main ways tenure becomes unattainable. More importantly as Esther Ohito reminds us, while there is no quantifiable data to show it, *we know*—Maria, Jane, I, and *you* know—that Black women and women of color are getting sick and dying in academia.

> Some of us decay as illnesses ingurgitate our bodies and psyches. Some of us occupy academic spaces in which our competence is continually questioned, and die slowly from inhaling the poisons emitted in those noxious environments (e.g., Esnard, 2019). Some of our bodies consume themselves as we attempt to claw our way into the "hegemonic centers of the academy," which "cannot be disentangled from the long historical apparatuses of genocidal and protogenocidal social organization" (Rodríguez, 2012, p. 812). Some of us, like June Jordan and Audre Lorde—who respectively taught at the University of California, Berkeley and the City University of New York's John Jay College of Criminal Justice and Hunter College—die cancerous deaths despite having earned academia's acknowledgements and accolades. Like Thea Hunter, a long-term adjunct who withered away in the academy's underbelly, some of us die and then decay—or conversely, decay and then die—with our ravenous hunger for legibility within the grammar of this network unsatiated (Harris, 2019). Some of us wilt and die bereft of recognition because academia starves our ways of living, knowing, and being (human)—and the associated ways of loving, hurting, healing, grieving, and surviving.[12]

The university is killing us. Our bodies are being sacrificed at the service of *their* "essential" project of diversity and inclusion.

Beyond tenure, another hurdle we face as scholars of color in academia, particularly if we work in ethnic studies fields, is the assumption that if our work focuses on minoritized communities we happen to be part of (as in Latinx scholars who are in Latinx studies), we are perceived as less serious and less scholarly. As one of my colleagues, a white woman, put in her evaluation of my work, "Your work is not scholarship, it's activism." Another pretty unique condition of academia is that all decisions about our careers, from being admitted into PhD programs to obtaining a job are made in great part by colleagues. The fact that, for many of us working in smaller interdisciplinary fields such as ethnic studies, our work is being appraised by faculty who are not equipped with the knowledge and tools to properly evaluate it means that the bias, racism, and ignorance of our colleagues shape our ability to succeed in traditional ways: getting a job, securing a promotion, publishing a book, obtaining a fellowship or grant, and receiving tenure. That was true in the case of Albert Laguna, an assistant professor of Latinx studies at Yale who was denied tenure in 2018 (though the case was eventually overturned thanks to the organizing efforts of students and faculty); of Paul Harris, an assistant professor of education at the University of Virginia whose tenure denial in 2019 was also reversed; and of Nikole Hannah-Jones, who was denied tenure by the University of North Carolina at Chapel Hill in 2021 despite her being a Pulitzer Prize–winning author and highly regarded in her field. Hannah-Jones's work was devalued and deemed suspect and politically motivated, due to both her race and her dedication to the study of Black histories. In all three cases, their work was read as inadequate, navel-gazing, and "narrow" by the mostly white non-expert faculty evaluating them for tenure.

While the process of soliciting reviews by experts in the field is meant to yield anonymous and adequate evaluation of a particular candidate's worth, in many cases, these external letters are dismissed, particularly if the recommenders are also faculty of color. The evaluation and outcome of the tenure review process demonstrates not only the ingrained institutional bias against faculty of color but also the ignorance of faculty in traditional fields in judging interdisciplinary work, work focusing on race and racial justice, and work that engages minoritized communities of color. My own research, which centers Black Latinidad, was described as "too narrow" by a colleague in the ad hoc committee that overturned my department's recommendation for tenure in 2019—in a department in which people typically dedicate their lives to studying the very narrow subject of a single author. Ironically, after my firing, a white man who writes about Black Latinx people in the same "narrow" field I work in was hired with tenure as the new expert in Latinx studies. Our fields, like our persons, are imagined as nonessential, even when our work in sustaining the university colonizing project of diversity and inclusion is proffered as essential.

Complicity with the colonizing project of the university is a requirement for tenure. To be part of the club—to belong—tenured faculty must believe and profess that the tenure process is indeed fair and impartial. Otherwise, they jeopardize their own success as tenured faculty. That is, admitting that the process of tenure and promotion is marred with biases, racism, discrimination, and ignorance and sustained through unequal and unfair labor systems based on racial capitalism and colonializing structures of exploitation and exclusion also means admitting that you benefited from this as others suffered. Decolonizing the university requires that people recognize their own complicity with the colonizing project of the university and make efforts to change those structures even when they benefit them. To decolonize the university, we would need to admit that our successes are not solely the reflection of our labor but also the result of institutional inequality.

While tenure is a very tangible example of the ways faculty become complicit with the university, there are many other ways this complicity is enacted daily. Take the case of Maria, mentioned above, as an example. The labor exploitation to which she was subjected directly benefited her colleagues, who were effectively relieved from that extra labor and therefore freed to pursue their research. That her classes were much larger on average meant she worked more than her colleagues, likely at a lower salary. Yet no one ever expressed discomfort with this unequal burden; nor did they raise their voice in support of compensating her for the extra work she was completing for the entire department. Rather, she was constantly asked to do more. After her departure from the university, Maria was replaced by another woman of color who left the department three years later due, in great part, to the exploitative labor practices that threatened her livelihood and hindered the chance of her obtaining tenure. These experiences are not unique. Maria's former department is not the only one that functions this way. Rather, the complicity that shaped the violence and exploitative practices Maria had to endure is systemic to the university as a colonizing space. That is, the university mimics the same dynamics of power and oppression that dominate the nation.

In the United States, these dynamics are, in turn, complicated by the US role as an empire across the world, and by its identity as a nation that became independent without securing the equality and freedom of all its people. Let's remember that slavery was abolished in the US eighty-nine years *after* independence. That is what changed—the masters, not the system. The colonial legacy that led to US independence without Black freedom; that sustained Jim Crow, the Chinese Exclusion Act, and Operation Wetback; and that allowed for the passage of the "Muslim travel ban," the caging of children at the US-Mexico border, and the murder of Black people at the hands of the police sustains the institutional structures of the modern university.

Colonial systems effectively divided humanity into two major categories: those who belong (typically white European men) and those who do not (everyone else). The end of every colonial regime—the white supremacist university included—requires rebellion.

Silence, the Accomplice

Silence in the face of injustice is often accompanied by words of consolation and support offered in private to the aggrieved party. This is another form of complicity. Over the years, as I spoke up during faculty or committee meetings or met with the administration about issues regarding admissions of students of color to graduate programs, inequality in hiring practices, the lack of ethnic studies programs, the need to support undocumented students, and many more injustices on campus, I was often unaccompanied in my task. Afterward, however, someone would unfailingly come up to me and say encouragingly, "I am so glad you raised that issue" or "What so-and-so said to you at that meeting was so awful." In 2014, during a meeting about graduate student admission,the faculty was asked to address a letter from mostly white graduate students who were asking the program to make a bigger effort to admit students of color. White senior faculty sat around the table in the large seminar room. The three women of color affiliates and all the graduate students had to sit on the periphery in the back of the room. When the meeting started, one of the faculty members—a white man who was a former department chair—raised his voice excitedly to defend the whiteness of the student body. "We have tried to admit them [students of color]," he said, "but what can we do if the *quality of mind* is not there?" (emphasis added). When I asked him to explain what exactly "quality of mind" means, he went on to state that graduate students of color were interested only in "racial issues and the present," adding, "How many students studying Black and brown suffering can we actually admit?" While there was so much I wanted to say to my racist colleague, I fell silent. The shock of his blatant racism overtook my body. I became sick and vomited at the meeting. I still believe this was probably the most appropriate response.

Many memories stuck with me after that meeting: the use of the phrase "quality of mind," which I would hear over and over and would always make me gag; the visual narrative of the room in which we three women of color faculty members were seated in the back, never invited to share our thoughts, even when the topic under discussion was the students we were serving and the future students of color who, if admitted, we would undoubtedly be asked to serve; but most of all, what stuck with me was the silence of my colleagues—their passivity and complicity with the former chair's racism. After the meeting, some colleagues wrote to offer their "support" or express dissent with his opinion. They wanted to assure me that they were not (as) racist. But these assurances were offered in private. Rarely did these colleagues raise their voices in public. This public silence and private support is a form of complicity. Silence is violence. As long as faculty members stand up to injustices and racism alone or in tiny numbers, they will continue to occur. If the administration can count on the complicit silence of faculty, the structures of inequality will remain untouched. Complicity sustains these structures.

One of the main ways through which the university makes faculty its accomplices is through silencing, including confidentiality in evaluation, hiring, tenure, and promotion structures. When I was denied tenure, I was not offered a single explanation why. After spending eight years working for an institution, getting excellent teaching evaluations, and carrying out an active and successful research agenda, I checked all the boxes of a successful tenure case. My chair and dean had assured me that my case was as picture perfect as it got. The news of my denial shocked everyone but me. I had never trusted the system; I had always expected something would go wrong, because as a woman of color in academia I had been trained to do so. I had fully expected my "quality of my mind" to be called into question. What I was not prepared for was for the silence of my colleagues. Only a handful of colleagues raised their voices and shared with me all the information they had access to; everyone else stayed silent. They privately expressed their outrage to me and offered their sympathies, but they refused to become *my* accomplices, instead upholding their loyalty to the university. One colleague—whom I had called a friend and who sat in the room where the decision about my tenure was made—ghosted me and never again answered my phone calls or emails. Another colleague, a woman of color, who had also sat in the room, admitted she knew what had transpired and that it was "fucked up and racist" but would not share information with me about the process. I tried for a year to understand exactly how the decision was made. I knew the reason was my "strangeness." I knew that as a Black Latina who was outspoken against the colonizing structures of the university, I had become dangerous and needed to be expunged. But I wanted to know more. I wanted to know which of my colleagues had made the decision and the official rationale. My colleagues who knew these things stayed silent. They were accomplices to my firing. Silence helps sustain the colonizing, racist, exclusionary structures of the elite university.

In early spring 2021 I was asked to speak to a group of faculty members at a small Latinx-serving institution about navigating academia as a person of color on the tenure track. The conversation was one of the most heartbreaking of my career. It was an intimate setting with fewer than a dozen faculty members, most of them Latinx and Black women. The conversation, which was supposed to last one hour, extended to over three. Everyone had questions. Every question came with a story; some came with tears. We all cursed and sighed as we recognized ourselves in every story. One Afro

Latina assistant professor shared that she had been made to teach extra courses to cover the sabbatical leave of her senior colleague, essentially doubling her teaching load without additional compensation. A Black lecturer shared that her colleagues expected her to do clerical work for them, like photocopying and running errands, in addition to teaching and advising. Words like "abusive," "violent," and "racist" were used to describe institutional structures and the white senior colleague accomplices sustaining them. After the catharsis, tears, cursing, and laughter, one of the faculty members asked me, "How do you make your colleagues understand the importance of our work? How can you make them care? I want them to care about our students! I want them to see what we are doing!" Everyone nodded.[13] As I stared at the group, one thing was clear to me: we are a very tired bunch. Our exhaustion is ancestral. Living in the United States in the context of a pandemic—living "in the wake," as scholar Christina Sharpe calls it—mourning our losses and forced to defer our full lives, constantly trying to survive antiblackness and white supremacy, living in these racialized bodies that are constantly made to unbelong, are insurmountable tasks, and we are tired.[14] We should not have to live like this. Many of us became scholars because we hoped to contribute to knowledge that would help change the inequality in our country and our world. Discovering that, rather than being the place where this is possible, academia is simply a microcosm of everything that is wrong with the world, is heartbreaking. Those of us who are parents and aunties to Black and brown children know we must teach them very early on how to survive out there: how to stay safe and grounded, how to care for their hearts and bodies. As scholars of color, we need to do the same with ourselves, we need to be our own aunties. We also need to do this for our junior colleagues and graduate students. We need to remind ourselves to take care, be safe, be cautious, find our tribe, watch out for the accomplices, not become an accomplice to the system that destroys us, and look out for our hearts. We are exhausted, and the road is too long and often too lonely. We cannot survive academia without accompaniment.

And yet, for a lot of us—particularly first-generation graduate students and faculty of color—the road to finding our community is slow and tortuous. It often takes years of trial and error, enduring institutional violence in silence. As graduate students, we do not always find mentors who support us. Even when we work with sympathetic professors, being first-generation and Black or brown and poor means we start our journey on foot while others ride aboard a train. It means that there is so much we don't know. We often don't know even where to start our journey to learn about the profession. We make many mistakes, and our mistakes are often misunderstood as stemming from a lack of interest or discipline, laziness, or another personal deficit. While I had many kind professors throughout graduate school who genuinely wanted me to succeed, I often experienced isolation and embarrassment in my interactions with them. It's not only that I didn't have answers but also that I didn't even know what questions to ask. When I graduated from the University of Michigan with a PhD in American studies, I was utterly unprepared for the academic world. I had not gone on the job market, nor did I really know how to. I didn't know how to contact academic presses or go about publishing articles. I had no idea what was waiting for me on the other side. I had a PhD, and yet I didn't really know what to do with it. I felt lost. Many people share similar experiences. Mentoring first-generation students of color is an important, difficult, and incredibly rewarding experience. It requires knowledge, patience, empathy, and compassion. It requires that professors avoid assumptions about students and instead ask questions to educate themselves. Over the years, as I made it my goal to support first-generation students, I've found myself crying with them, offering line-by-line revisions of their work, paying for airplane tickets, and buying suits for interviews and other necessities out of pocket. Mentoring these students required me to show my own vulnerabilities and allow my students to guide me through how to support them rather than assuming I knew what they needed. It is the most incredible exchange—a huge responsibility—and the greatest honor of my career. Accompanying my students as they learn and unlearn has also been a way to build community and create spaces that sustain me.

After I graduated from Michigan, I was fortunate enough to receive a Future of Minority Studies fellowship at Syracuse University. I was hosted by the Department of Women's and Gender Studies. For six months, I was surrounded by the care and mentorship of feminist and BIPOC scholars, including Chandra Talpade Mohanty, Linda Carty, and Silvio Torres-Saillant. They held my hand and helped me through my insecurities and my profound ignorance of the profession, and they gave me sincere and thoughtful feedback that put me on the right path to becoming the scholar I am now. Their support and kindness also modeled for me the kind of teacher and mentor I hoped to become. Their accompaniment showed me that, indeed, another way is possible.

That same year, upon applying for an assistant professor position, and due to a glitch in the electronic submission system, I received a copy of a recommendation letter written on my behalf by one of my professors at Michigan—a white man. The way he described me was eye-opening. In his letter, he wrote, "Lorgia comes from the ghetto. That she has managed to overcome the violence, poverty, and shame of her background and finished a dissertation is already a great accomplishment." The fact that my professor saw me as a kid "from the ghetto" for whom academia was an unattainable space had put a huge distance between us and made it difficult for me to connect with him intellectually and otherwise. Reading his letter was so liberating. For years I had blamed myself for not knowing all that I did not know. I had felt ashamed for not knowing how to cultivate the kind of relationships I saw some of my graduate student friends having with their professors. I always felt like a bother and a burden, which made it so hard for me to ask for help. Reading the recommendation letter from my white professor allowed me to see that the wedge that divided us, and that ultimately made it so I left graduate school without fully understanding what academia was and what my role would be in it, was caused by my "strangeness." He could not see me or my scholarship beyond my background because, to him, people like me could not belong. Who I was in their eyes—a kid "from the ghetto," an immigrant, a poor person—determined how far they thought I could get. Completing the dissertation was enough, maybe even too much, for a kid from the ghetto.

Years later I shared the letter with a senior Latinx studies scholar friend. She reminded me that the project of "diversity and inclusion" is precisely to produce us as "kids from the ghetto" and only as that because it facilitates the narrative of the white savior. It allows the university to pat itself on the back and feel proud of its so-called inclusion while it sustains the structures of inequality that perpetuate the wedge between my professor and me—between them and us. My professor's assessment of me as a ghetto kid encapsulated me within the framework of diversity and inclusion, reducing me to a commodity, an exotic figure, while my intellectual contributions remained unacknowledged. His reading of my person as a kid from the ghetto summons the violence of scientific racism. It is a twenty-first-century manifestation of cranial measurement.

Being essentialized as the kid from the ghetto was a reminder that somehow my admission into a graduate program or my being hired into an academic job is *different*: it is not the result of my "quality of mind" but rather a sort of charity plan to create "inclusion." We are assumed to be incompetent from the moment we arrive.

That is, inequity precedes our insertion in academia. Along with the elitist, white supremacist, and exclusionary project of "diversity," it predetermines how we are mentored, how our work is read, and whether people in power invest in our futures. The way this plays out in real life for many graduate students is very tangible: they are denied fellowships, they are not offered the most rewarding teaching opportunities, and at times they do not even find out about possibilities and options in their particular fields of study.

So, how do we survive academia as first-generation scholars of color? How do we find community amid this violence? And, to paraphrase one of my colleagues during the faculty meeting I was invited to lead in spring 2021, how do we make them (our white colleagues) care?

To have community, we must commune. That is, we must insist on *community* as an action, as a verb. Despite the tortuous road, along the way I have found *my* accomplices in the fight to decolonize the university: colleagues outside my institution who read my work, listened, and encouraged me to keep going, who generously shared their own stories of struggles and survival and had my back when the university didn't. It takes work, building spaces, creating room, and allowing ourselves to be vulnerable and honest. Communities can be big or small, elaborate or simple. Some of the communities I have helped build consist of the simple practice of breaking bread together. I cook for people, open my home to them, and allow them to be with each other, sharing space and care. Other spaces require institutional building and support. I organize small symposia, conferences, and workshops aimed at supporting young scholars of color. I host writing groups. In time, these efforts have paid off. They have allowed me to build networks and communities of accomplices who would readily fight with me. That is how we survive, thrive, and fight back. That is how we rebel. However, finding these networks takes time. It is often difficult, particularly for people in smaller, more isolated environments. It requires entrusting our work—and at times our hearts—to people we often don't know well, in the hope that they are "one of us." It is a risk, but it is one worth taking. We must find a way forward that allows for more public opportunities to create networks of support—particularly for young scholars and graduate students—in which information can be shared and kinship and collegiality can flourish. For those of us who are tenured, who are secure in our jobs, this means we must take the lead not only in calling out complicity with violence where we see it, but also in creating alternative spaces—physical, virtual, emotional, and intellectual—to sustain us. The road is long, so we need to stop and recharge, to rest in order to continue walking.

We cannot force our colleagues to be allies; we cannot make them see what is right in front of their eyes but they refuse to acknowledge. But we can insist that our labor becomes visible, acknowledged, and compensated. For that, we need to be like the thieves in my dad's movies. We need to find our people, and together we need to take the resources available to us through our institutions and use them to build spaces that sustain us. That is how we make it. That is how we thrive. We also need to work together in community to create effective boycotting practices, to come up with sustainable ways to withhold and leverage our labor when necessary. We need to say no to institutional work on "diversity and inclusion" committees, as by now we know what that labor entails and that it never translates into action that actually benefits our students or faculty of color. We can say no to serving as The One—lending legitimacy via our representation—to what is essentially a project of exclusion. When we do decide to serve, we need to leverage our service, quantify our work, and demand compensation. We can do this, for example, by requiring time off from teaching in exchange for service. Insisting on the value of our service is critical to ending the cycle of exploitation. Saying yes to exploitative labor does not guarantee tenure, institutional recognition, or belonging. Maria, Jane, and I know this all too well. Our labor is what the university wants and needs; we must withhold it and leverage it if we are not respected.

In academia, as in the world, we are *still* experiencing the afterlives of slavery and colonialism; the lasting effects of systems of oppression that have never fully been eradicated from our societies and our institutions. We are *still* dealing with systemic violence against Black and Indigenous people and people of color. We are seeing how this violence extends to immigrants of color across the globe, producing them as subhuman and unworthy of care and dignity. We know how the afterlives of these systems continue to silence minoritized voices from all public discourses, while also perpetuating economic disparity and environmental injustice. Take the COVID-19 pandemic as an example: statistics show us that Black, Indigenous, and Latinx people are dying at higher rates and have higher risks of infection than white people.[15] Inequality is so ingrained in our institutions that people have become comfortable with the idea that our lives should be casualties, and we are being asked to wait for change, to be patient for the deferred solutions that are coming. But Black, brown, and Indigenous oppressed people are tired of waiting for justice, and we have become more and more aware that justice cannot be served, for example, by jailing one racist policeman after one of us is murdered while the systemic violence continues to endanger our lives. The justice we need cannot be attained through individual reparation. It is not sufficient. It doesn't do anything for our deferred genocide, for halting the inequality that persistently puts our lives in precarious conditions, or the violence that separates us at the borders of humanity.

We tend to think about civil rights as an era that has passed and romanticize the sixties as a moment of arrival. But the reality is that for many of us BIPOC living in the Global North, the fight for civil and human rights is still ongoing. The fights we thought we might have won are still being fought albeit in different arenas, perhaps by different actors. As we continue to fight for our civil rights, for our rights to live and not just survive, we don't need the people in power to pretend to listen. We don't need thoughts and prayers, or the university equivalent, "the memoradum of support." What we need are different structures. What we need is a shift in power to restore balance so that we can guarantee no more Black lives are destroyed, that no more people are dispossessed and that no more migrants are treated as subhuman. That is the moment in which we find ourselves, both in the streets and inside the university. And while we must protest—while we must demand and fight for justice—we must also create alternative spaces to sustain us within and outside our institutions. If I have learned anything over the past decade, it is to not trust institutions—to not believe in the systems that were never meant to sustain me. It is an insurmountable task to work, care, teach, and produce knowledge while living and working in this violence. And yet we do, and we must. We must also find other ways, though. We must also create our own collectives of joy and learning where our work and our lives are properly recognized as essential.

As scholars and teachers fighting for our lives against the structural death our institutions sustain, we need to find our own accomplices in our students. For that, we need to stop being complicit with the silencing structures of the colonizing university. We need to share information, stories, and knowledge. For many of us teaching first-generation students of color, we know how much our students rely on us—on our support and allyship. Often, they ask us to do more than we can do. They do so because there is no one else, because as The One, we are all they have. Educate them. Model boundaries. Show them you care, but also show them that you are human, and that you are tired. Say no, and follow that no with an explanation of why not that paints a clear picture of the institutional constraints that limit your ability to participate in every single event you are invited to. Think carefully about your syllabus and your assignments. Be intentional in your teaching and generous in the classroom. Give them the tools with which to decolonize the university by showing them the ways in which it attempts to colonize them/us.

Over the years, students have built a home for me in institutional spaces that did not otherwise sustain me. It is for my students I fight; it is for them I rebel in community. I strive to model for them how to be intentional, how to think about the work we do as part of this world. This is especially critical when working with graduate students who will become the next generation of faculty of color at the mercy of the institution—unless we give them the tools with which to rebel.

3.

MIDTERM

Teaching as Accompaniment

I come from a long line of rebellious women. Fearless women. Warrior women. Feminist women. Perhaps they would not have called themselves feminists—a label that in the Dominican Republic, for the entire twentieth century, was associated either with formal political party organizing or with "foreign" white women.[1] Their feminism was simpler, quieter, and more tacit. It revolved around mutual care for each woman in the community through daily practices of support and presence.

A big family secret is that after seeing her sister suffer at the hands of her abusive husband, my great-grandmother Julia organized all the women in her village. They came up with a singing code they would employ while washing clothes on the riverbanks if they were at the receiving end of abuse. They weaponized their knowledge of herbs to aid sleep by adding them to their husbands' teas and meals. Most of all, they promised to care for each other and come to each other's aid in times of need. Their rebellion worked. No sooner did a man become abusive than five women would come to defend her. They did not use their hands or try to fight the aggressor. Rather, they would surround the house while singing loudly, making their presence noticeable. The abuser would be so perplexed by the sudden external attention that he would stop. After a while the community began to recognize the singing as an alarm, and even some men in the village began to participate, interrupting the violence.

A rumor spread that the Peña women were rebellious. Perhaps it is because of their rebelliousness that many of my great-aunts never married, and others moved away. Still, my grandfather would tell me with pride that his mother was *una dura*, a strong woman. He was proud to see her in me.

One of the challenges of academia for me has been understanding how to use my feminist power—how to be *una dura*—in the face of violence. Academia's power resides precisely in its exclusivity and exclusion. Knowledge, as imagined by the university, is measured by its proximity to particular notions of civility that are grounded, as the work of Lisa Lowe, Sylvia Wynter, and many others have shown, on the Eurocentric, colonial, patriarchal, heteronormative, and white supremacist understanding of the world. Yet we continue to reproduce and value that scale, rejecting—consciously or not—all other epistemologies: the feminism of my great-grandmother, the praxis and philosophy of the many Black, Indigenous, brown, and Asian *dura* women of the world. To be in the university as women of color, as women from colonized nations, as migrants, is to be in tension with ourselves. It is a position of discomfort. To be in academia and remain *una dura*, we need to be comfortable existing within discomfort, never aiming to belong or conform, for conformity is another form of death. To conform to academia is to renounce our collective project of being and belonging. Our strategy, therefore, must be to find ways to return the discomfort through a feminist praxis of being, knowing, and doing.

I am an Afro Latina immigrant woman from the Caribbean. I came to the United States at the age of twelve, making me what some call "first generation and a half," or *con un pie aquí y otro allá* (with one foot here and the other one there). Like so many other immigrant kids, I went to college with a desire to improve the socio-economic status of my family. In the process, however, that desire transformed into something bigger. As I took class after class and found nothing that reflected my experience or my history, I became more and more aware of the gap between academia and my community. That distance became even more evident as I entered graduate school, as my socioeconomic status, immigrant background, race, the fact that I was an English-language learner, the fact that I had not had the same opportunities other kids had, all marked me as different. In many ways, these things defined my unbelonging to the university. I had two choices: I could try to fit in, or I could try to change the structures of exclusion that made it so my history was not in books. Like my great-grandmother, I chose rebellion.

My academic path has been profoundly personal. It has been paved by my peoples' experiences of exclusion from books, institutions, and the very nation in which I live. It has also been highly communal, grounded in the feminism of my great-grandmother and aunties with a desire for justice for the communities I grew up in: immigrant, poor, and Black and with a very stubborn but radically hopeful conviction that education can and should be transformative—otherwise, what is the point of teaching or studying? My journey to obtaining a PhD, becoming a professor, to teaching, and to engaged scholarship, was grounded in my commitment to social justice and to finding answers to questions that emerged from my experience as an Afro Latina immigrant from the Dominican Republic confronting everyday racism and sexism in the United States. Social justice was and is both the method and the impetus for my journey through Latinx and ethnic studies, guiding my writing and my teaching.

I am often asked how I balance activism and academic work. I don't. My rebellion—my social justice work, scholarship, and teaching—are intrinsically linked. I see my academic work and teaching as liberatory practices. My research seeks to contradict the silences and erasures of *my* history from books and archives. My teaching is a hopeful exercise of freedom-making. I teach in and for freedom. My scholarship and teaching are my ways to confront the aggressors, as did my great-grandmother. They are how I honor her legacy.

On October 14, 2010, shortly after beginning my first job as an assistant professor of Latinx studies at the University of Georgia, Athens (UGA), the Georgia Board of Regents voted 14–2 "to prohibit the top public universities from enrolling students without papers in any school that has rejected other qualified applicants for the past two years because of lack of space."[2] The policy, which keeps academically qualified students from attending the top five public research universities in the state, was based on the belief that undocumented students were taking seats in the public university system that rightly belonged to citizens. However, a study conducted by the very same board of regents found that undocumented students make up less than 0.2 percent of all public university students; most undocumented students are enrolled in technical and community colleges.[3]

Parallel to the regents' ban, the state of Georgia introduced one of the toughest anti-immigrant bills in the nation, House Bill 87 in April 2011, which required law enforcement officers to inquire about immigration status during routine stops for minor traffic violations and hand over any undocumented suspects to federal authorities.[4] The bill also required most employers to check immigration status through the federal E-Verify database, and it stipulates possible prison sentences for those convicted of knowingly harboring or transporting undocumented residents. While the "show me your papers" provisions of HB 87 and similar laws in other states resulted in civil liberties lawsuits and injunctions by federal judges, ending in the eventual dismissal of the provisions, insufficient attention was given to the move by the UGA Board of Regents to deny undocumented students access to state universities and colleges.

The news shocked me like a bucket of ice water. How do you even ban people from accessing *public* education? Isn't the whole point of public education to make it accessible to everyone? As a new professor, a Latina teaching Latinx studies to Latinx students, and someone who was once undocumented and who comes from a mixed-status family, I was not prepared for this news. At the time, I was teaching the Introduction to Latino/a Studies class, the course with the largest enrollment in my department. Shortly after the ban was announced, Latinx students began to disappear from my class. Undocumented students were simply too afraid to come to class. Some decided to migrate north with their families in search of more security. Amid this crisis, one of my students, a twenty-year-old Mexican American man, came to see me during office hours. He wanted to say goodbye. He would not be returning in the fall, as his family was headed to upstate New York. They were all afraid of being deported. When he left my office, I closed the door and cried. It was a cathartic, ugly cry. I didn't understand. Hadn't we elected Obama to avoid this kind of disaster? He had promised to pass the DREAM Act and halt deportation. How did we get here? After a few minutes of crying, I wiped the tears from my face, stepped out of my office, and began to organize. Clearly, the state of Georgia had expected a quiet response from the population about the state's exclusion and expulsion of undocumented people. Instead, students and faculty began to organize to reverse the policy.

Organizing in academia is a tricky, messy, and incredibly irritating process. It requires patience and the translation of rhetoric into action. Luckily, I found a small group of women professors—or rather, they found me: Betina Kaplan, Bethany Moreton, and Pamela Voekel. They had even less patience than I did, and together we were able to think and act in what philosopher Jonathan Lear calls "radical hope," believing in the potential to enact effective change.[5] We started to circulate petitions, write letters, and organize teach-ins. We looked for ways to create dialogue, bring attention to the issue, and most importantly, pressure the UGA administration to reverse its ban. It soon became evident, though, that nothing we could do within the system would be enough to reverse the policy. Yet, the everyday realities for undocumented communities were too pressing to simply wait for structural and institutional changes. So we began to build outside the structures.

A University of Freedom

I remember the exact moment when Freedom University was born. Some memories are imprinted in one's mind like tattoos. I can close my eyes and see everyone's faces—people I didn't know yet who would become *my* people for a lifetime. Most of all, I remember Keish Kim. She was this young, smart, incredibly honest undocumented youth organizer from Atlanta who had come to Athens for the meeting at our request. Pam, Betina, Bethany, and I had reached out to local immigrant organizations, including the newly founded Georgia Undocumented Youth Alliance (GUYA), of which Keish was a cofounder. GUYA had guts. They had been staging civil disobedience actions, blocking streets, demanding an end to the ban. We wanted to help, but we didn't know how. Sure, we wrote petitions and letters and did the academic thing, talking to deans, provosts, and university councils, eventually earning a significant amount of support. But there was also an immediate concern for the lives of students who were affected by this inhumane legislation. Academic organizing is slow, and it pauses during the summer months when the school year ends. GUYA, though, was not on pause. We reached out, and Keish came to us with her beautiful story, her *ganas* (desire and will) and her radical hope for a better way. And in the simplest and most brilliant way, she challenged us. "What can we do to support you?" we asked, to which she answered: "You are teachers, right? Teach!"

Inspired in great part by the bravery of GUYA, and in conversation with local immigrant organizations, students, and community members, we came up with the idea for creating a "third space." This idea of a third space emerged during a meeting with Beto, a local undocumented activist and community leader. With his help, and that of the Georgia Students for Public Higher Education, the Economic Justice Coalition, and other individuals, we were able to reach students, find community partners, raise funds, buy books, and obtain a donated space. The creation of a board of advisers, composed of nationally renowned scholars, activists, leaders, and writers, opened many doors and provided the necessary moral support in the beginning stages of community organizing. Within weeks, admission applications from undocumented students started pouring in. We had students, we had four committed faculty members, many volunteers, a donated space, and most importantly, we had *ganas*—the will to do it.

Freedom University Georgia was born!

On October 9, 2011, Freedom University Georgia opened its doors to thirty-two undocumented students in Athens. Since its conception, Freedom University has contributed to a recent movement that is redefining struggles in the US South, bringing together scholars, community organizations, students, DREAMers (undocumented people who migrated to the US as children), and undocumented immigrants from diverse backgrounds in a coalition of rebellious freedom fighters. The first day of classes was emotional for everyone involved. Out of the corner of my eye, I saw some students crying and others grinning with excitement at the sight of a room packed with DREAMers. One of our students, GUYA activist Gustavo Madrigal-Piña, kept saying, "These are students! These are students! We have a school!" The bond among students was almost immediate. In our scholarly minds, we thought we were creating an educational space where students who wanted to could indeed learn. We had worked very hard on the syllabus, the assignments, and the academic preparation, in addition to the logistics of the organization.

Professor Pam Voekel, Freedom University cofounder, and students, October 2011

However, that very first day it became evident to everyone involved that Freedom University was so much more than a school. Our students, for the first time in their lives, found themselves surrounded by a community of people who shared their own struggles and dreams. Their immigration status was no longer a secret to be guarded but the very reason they found themselves in this wonderful space. Their shared experience guided their commitment to Freedom University, their classes, and their own academic goals.

I like sharing this birth story not only because it is, in many ways, the story of my own birth as a rebellious teacher but also because that mandate—"Teach!"—has followed me for a decade, shaping my teaching philosophy, my time in the classroom, and my engagement with critical ethnic studies as a site of knowledge and a method of teaching and thinking. What does it mean to teach as Keish mandated? What does it mean to teach for freedom? I think about this question often as I work on my teaching and as new generations of college students arrive with different needs and contexts. Teaching for freedom means making the classroom a space for rebellion against systemic exclusion, racism, and oppression. If we take that mandate seriously, everything we do—from the construction of the syllabus to how we interact with our students—would guide us to create a learning environment that is transformative. In "Teaching Community: A Pedagogy of Hope," bell hooks wrote:

> We need mass-based political movements calling citizens of this nation to uphold democracy and the rights of everyone to be educated, and to work on behalf of ending domination in all its forms—to work for justice, changing our educational system so that schooling is not the site where students are indoctrinated to support imperialist white-supremacist capitalist patriarchy or any ideology, but rather where they learn to open their minds, to engage in rigorous study and to think critically.[6]

Through her life and teachings, hooks modeled this pedagogy for us. She taught us that education is an act of radical justice, and that the classroom can be a space from which redress, abolition, and decolonizing practices can be learned. To do so, teachers and students must, hooks reminds us, bring an open mind; I add, we also need an open heart. We must be willing to be vulnerable and to accept individual failures and mistakes to make room for collective learning, collective freedom, collective joy.

One of the classes I teach regularly is Performing Latinidad, a course I developed at the beginning of my career and that has become a sort of sanctuary for first-generation students of color. I have spoken and written often about this course because of the immense impact it has had in both my teaching and my activism within the university.[7] Neither UGA nor Harvard, like many other institutions across the United States, has a department, program, or center for ethnic studies. They do not provide students of color with a meeting space or a venue for community events. For many students of color, the classroom—and particularly the ethnic studies classroom—has become such a space.[8]

In my Latinx studies courses, students meet each other and build alliances and networks that allow them to confront the violence and racism of their environment. Students enrolled in my Latinx studies classes have organized to create publications, form organizations, and build communities beyond the classroom. The first course of its kind in any of the institutions I have taught, Performing Latinidad examines the constructions, imaginings, and representations of Latinidad as performed in a variety of genres, including poetry, fiction, drama, music, slam, and film, in conversation with various sociocultural movements that have helped define notions of US Latinx identities. By bringing into conversation Latinx studies criticism, border theories, Chicana feminism, and race and ethnicity theory, we address issues of identity, citizenship, language authenticity, representation, and belonging.

Because the class has a hands-on performance and art-making component, it is also incredibly engaging for students of all levels (from first-year undergraduates to doctoral students). Every semester, the students enrolled in Performing Latinidad have worked with a visiting artist to develop an artistic intervention based on readings from the class. Students look forward to their final group projects, as the performances are some of the rare instances in which Latinx students of all races become visible on a campus that seems to constantly make invisible its students and faculty of color. They work in groups, meet outside class, build physical artistic structures, rehearse their interventions, and at the end of the semester, take over the entire University Yard, visually and sonically.

Altar to Saint J.Lo, Harvard University Yard, 2015

Over the years, I secured funding to invite artists and activists to coteach with me sections of the course for periods of two to eight weeks. The experiences of coteaching and art-making in the class are invaluable. To be able to sustain a semester-long relationship with students and to work with them for weeks at a time was a meaningful experience for both the artists and the students. While not every institution has the budget to provide the kind of intervention I was able to create in my classroom, I must note that in every teaching situation, from Freedom University to Harvard, I have strived to create that kind of environment for students, working with local artists and fundraising in any possible way (from selling tamales and cupcakes to writing grants) to make this collaboration possible.

In 2015, for example, students enrolled in my course at Harvard erected an altar to "Saint J.Lo" that became a shrine for ethnic studies "prayers" and *ofrendas*. Letters and notes asked Saint J.Lo to intercede on behalf of Latinx students in asking "Mr. Harvard" to finally provide a space for Latinx students, approval for a concentration and a department, and the hiring of professors in the field of ethnic studies. The shrine became a site of activism and representation for Latinx and other students of color on campus who guarded it and brought flowers, candles, and other offerings to ask for the *milagro* (the miracle). The shrine remained in place for over a week due to the complicit relationship between Latinx students and the custodial staff charged with removing it.[9]

A year later, during the 2016 presidential campaign, the students enrolled in Performing Latinidad decided that the theme for the final performance was going to be "taco trucks on every corner of Harvard Yard." This performance challenged the then popular controversial statement by Marco Gutiérrez, cofounder of Latinos for Trump: "If you don't do something about it [immigration], you're going to have taco trucks on every corner."[10] Over the fall semester, under the direction of performance artist Josefina Báez, each of the six groups prepared an installation and a performative text based on class readings that spoke to both the overarching topic of the class and the specific intervention (taco trucks) they had chosen. Báez was able to participate as a visiting fellow in our course and support the art-making for a period of two weeks. To make this possible I secured a grant that paid for her honorarium and travel. Báez often commented on how unique and exciting this experience was as she got to get to know each of the students and work with them to help them realize their own projects. Rather than come and read or perform for a crowd of students, the experience of cocreating allowed for a sense of intimacy and made the work all the more impactful. With guidance from Báez, students built cardboard trucks that moved throughout the campus, sharing "poetry tacos" with passersby. Students wrote original texts, made installations on trees, and even transformed the iconic John Harvard statue into a "bad hombre," challenging the rhetoric of the Trump campaign as well as the language of Harvard's administration that continued to refuse the creation of a Latinx studies department, despite thirty years of student demand. As we walked through the yard during the ninety-minute collective performance, students, faculty, tourists, and passersby joined us.[11] Some were curious, others touched. I remember that year one interaction in particular with a brown Latinx woman who was a student in the Divinity School. She walked behind me, sobbing for a good part of the performance. At the end, she introduced herself as a Latina from El Paso. She thanked me for making her feel seen for the first time in her four years as a student, asked me for a hug, and left. I have thought often about this student, whom I never saw again, how our little interruption of daily life on campus transformed hers, how our little rebellion gave her community.

Students drive a "poetry taco truck" around campus as a poetry procession follows

Josefina Báez (left), Lorgia García Peña, and students debriefing after a taco truck performance

The performative taco trucks intervention bridged the larger national political climate with the local campus climate, exposing the hypocrisy of the university in its refusal to recognize Latinx studies as a legitimate field of inquiry while simultaneously celebrating its strides in diversity. Much like the national politics that professed interest in the "Latinx vote" without pausing to understand Latinidad, Latinx diversity, and the needs of the multiple communities that embrace that label, the university upheld a narrative of diversity and inclusion, sustained by statistics on admission, all the while ignoring the needs of student population and the field that represents them. And yet, despite the violence and erasure, the energy my students brought to campus during the performance was contagious. It was a triumphant day, and everyone felt elated about the work they had done. The morning of the next class meeting, in which we were supposed to unpack the work done, we woke up to the news that Donald Trump had been elected president.

That Wednesday morning, I struggled with the decision of whether to cancel class, as many of my colleagues had done. It was an overwhelming day—a day of mourning and a scary day for many of the mostly Black, brown, queer, and undocumented students enrolled in Performing Latinidad. I simply did not have any words of comfort or wisdom that could assuage their fears, even a little. As I searched for an answer in my syllabus as to what to do that day in class, I stumbled upon Barbara Tomlinson and George Lipsitz's essay "American Studies as Accompaniment." In it, the authors argue that scholars need to "know the work we want our work to do and how our scholarship can serve to accompany positive changes in our society" if we want to actually dismantle the oppressive systems that persistently reproduce inequality and oppression in times of terror and repression.[12] They write,

> Centrally important to the success of our scholarly endeavors is *knowing the work we want our work to do*, taking responsibility for the world we are creating through our endeavors, for the ways of being in the world that we are modeling and promoting. The work of American studies can be organized around the concept of *accompaniment*. Accompaniment is a disposition, a sensibility, and a pattern of behavior. It is both a commitment and a capacity that can be cultivated. Two metaphors of accompaniment are particularly relevant: 1) accompaniment as participating with and augmenting a community of travelers on a road; 2) accompaniment as participating with others to create music. Thinking about American studies in terms of these acts of accompaniment can promote new ways of knowing and new ways of being that can equip scholars.[13] (emphasis added)

The work I want my teaching to do, the reason I became a teacher, is to enact social change: to create the kind of classroom that had been denied to me, a first-generation Black Latina daughter of immigrants from Trenton, New Jersey. My commitment to my students was thus grounded in justice and a hope for the impact I want students to have in their communities. So that day, instead of canceling class, I opened my classroom to all students who needed a place to process what it meant for them to now be forced to live in a Trumpian world. I decided to accompany them, trusting that the community we had worked to cocreate the past several months would hold us. As I stood in front of the lecture hall that morning, I was reminded once again of the power of community. Students came in holding each other; many cried. And for the first forty minutes of class, we allowed ourselves to express our fear and anger, and to simply listen.

I did my best to make sure students felt safe in the classroom by setting the tone for respectful processing. At the beginning of class I made the following announcement: "If you voted for Trump or sympathize with his narrative and politics, this is simply not your space today. You may leave or sit silently. This is a safe space for people who may not feel safe anywhere else today. Nothing we say here today leaves the classroom." We had worked together to build trust and accountability in the classroom. My disclaimer was an echoing rather than a warning of what I knew everyone in the room deserved and wanted for that moment and space. There were many undocumented students enrolled in the course who woke up terrified that they would be deported or persecuted. My priority that day was to make sure they felt safe to speak if they chose to, at least for the duration of the class, that they felt seen and respected, knowing that at least for the next hour and a half they were safe. They did speak, and we all listened to their fears, their stories, and their sobs. Then I asked, "What now? What do we do in the space we inhabit here at Harvard to support our most vulnerable in our community? How do we *hope*, and how do we learn amid fear and terror? What is the work we need to do?"

What followed will stay with me forever: one student spontaneously got up and went to the board and began writing as her peers shared their thoughts and ideas. I sat down and watched my students take the lead in identifying the most urgent needs they saw in their community: protecting undocumented students. They continued working after class, and within three hours they had drafted a petition (which garnered over six thousand signatures in the course of three days) that would be adopted and adapted by colleges and universities across the United States, including Dartmouth College, Rutgers University, Tufts University, University of Pennsylvania, among many others, calling for university campuses to become "sanctuaries" to protect their undocumented peers from the violence that was to come.[14] Their actions—their accompaniment—went beyond the class; it extended for several years as they continued to organize and think together through writing, discussions, teach-ins, and eventually through rallies, civil disobedience, and media interventions. Their actions led to the founding of an organization in support of undocumented students, Protect Undocumented Students at Harvard (PUSH), and to the creation of several university resources, including staff positions and the allocation of financial resources for Deferred Action for Childhood Arrivals (DACA) renewal and legal fees. Recently, I reflected on those initial postelection days with a student who has since graduated and become a union organizer. We talked about what the experience meant for students like herself. She said, "The syllabus gave us the tools, and the class gave us the community. The method for organizing was always in the class."

A PUSH student demonstration on the steps of Widener Library at Harvard University, November 2016

Social engagement and community-grounded learning have always been at the center of ethnic and Latinx studies efforts in the United States. The 1960s Chicanx student walkouts in the western US led to the founding of the first Chicanx studies program at California State University, Los Angeles, in 1968. In the 1970s, sit-ins and demonstrations in the Northeast also led to the formation of Puerto Rican and Hispanic Caribbean studies programs at Rutgers University, the City University of New York, with Hunter College being a particularly important site of organizing.[15] In the early twenty-first century, the actions of students at Williams College, Wellesley College, and Yale University resulted in the hiring of Latinx studies faculty; the creation of spaces, centers, and departments; and most importantly, the formation of alliances among faculty, students, and staff. Social justice is at the core of how we *do* Latinx studies. Yet, while we know that history, how this commitment translates to the everyday life of our students in the classroom is less evident, though not less important. The example of the postelection class session, inspiring as it is, is also exceptional. The political circumstances and campus environment in 2016, amid a dining-hall worker strike and the national elections, coupled with the performative nature of the class, allowed for expressive forms of activism that would have been impossible, or at least less natural, in a more traditional classroom and in a different political climate. What I want to highlight as a lesson for thinking about teaching *as freedom* is neither the performative political interventions of my students (from the rallies to the taco trucks) nor the administrative responses to their activism (the funding and staff support), but rather the more tacit elements that led to their working *together,* to what my student identified in her own reflection: the class as a method of social justice through *acompañamiento*/accompaniment.

The concept of "accompaniment" comes from Latin American liberation theory and activism. It relates to the idea that social change is a process that is not given to but emerges from the people. Allies cannot create social change alone; they cannot "bring" justice and equity to oppressed peoples, but they can accompany them in the struggle with patience and courage. They can participate in the creation of social change not only by recognizing their own privilege and complicity in the production of exclusionary systems but also by listening to how these experiences shape the everyday life of people at the receiving end of violence and exclusion.

Accompaniment opposes the traditional neoliberal racial-capitalist model of competitive labor markets and NGO-driven development in which "progress" is brought to a community rather than emerging from within it. This dominant model has failed in moments of crisis, even when those implementing it are well intentioned (as seen, for example, in the failure to reconstruct Haiti after the 2010 earthquake and the rebuilding of New Orleans post–

Hurricane Katrina). In this increasingly market-driven world, we are encouraged to think of ourselves as individual owners of our lives, identities, careers, and destinies. As such, we are each responsible for our own successes and failures. The dominant reward structures in this society cultivate competitiveness rather than cooperation and collective work. In the classroom, this often manifests in students' desire to shine during discussion, earn better grades, and protect their research and sense of authorship. We know that our work as scholars grows and becomes stronger through collective conversations with our peers and audiences. The same is true of active learning for students in the classroom.

To learn together, though, it is first necessary to trust one another. We must feel comfortable and secure in the space we inhabit in the classroom, knowing our ideas will never be dismissed as silly or stupid. We must appreciate the significance of rejecting the dominance of a single voice. This is not an easy task, as most students of color are survivors of deep classroom trauma. We have all been, at one point or another, the only one or one of few of our ethnicity or race. We have had to learn our own histories as side projects. We have been presumed to be experts and expected to speak for our ethnic or racial groups based solely on our experiences occupying racialized bodies. In fall 2021, during my first semester teaching at Tufts University, one of the students enrolled in my seminar on Black Latinidad, a person of color, told me during office hours that they felt overwhelmed in my class. As they spoke, tears kept falling. For a moment I panicked: were the assignments too demanding? Was it too much reading? Then it dawned on me, this student was not overwhelmed *by* my class, they were simply feeling safe enough to fall apart in my class.

As I asked them questions, they began to give words to all those feelings: trauma, shame, anger, fear, longing. It was the first time this student had had a professor of color. Despite having taken courses that focused on race, this was the first time they felt like they were part of a collective conversation that interrogated race rather than forced them to perform their race for white people. By the end of the term, after we learned as a community to speak openly and collectively about institutional trauma, this student made a self-assessment that was brilliant and painful. They wrote:

> For the first time in my four years of college, I was in the classroom where I felt seen. It was not only that the readings and the syllabus reflected back to me, but the classroom environment, the community our professor insisted on building, also saw me. I realized how used I was to not being seen. I felt naked at first and it was scary. Now I feel enraged that it took this long for someone to see me here at Tufts. I now want more.[16]

Over my almost two decades of teaching I collected numerous letters, notes, emails, even short video messages, from students expressing their gratitude for the shared space we cocreated in the classroom. But getting to this point in my teaching career was not something I was taught to do in graduate school. I never had a classroom like mine in college. I build my teaching praxis in *contradiction to*, against, how I had been forced to learn. The impulse to freedom came from institutional trauma.

How then can teachers create spaces of freedom in the classroom in ways that allow our students of color to move beyond trauma and pain and to cocreate justice and joy? How do we teach in/for freedom from within institutions that are built to imprison, erase us, and unbelong us? To commune, there must first be trust. To trust there must be hope for the possibility of healing.

To develop a trusting community in the classroom, I begin by acknowledging these traumas as I experienced them, while also inviting students to strive to create with me a different kind of learning environment. Together we agree on simple guidelines for respecting one another that go from not dominating the conversation to checking our own privileges and what in academia we call "the subject position" or simply put, our identities and place in the world, before posing questions. Additionally, there are three requirements that I include in all my courses: (1) Everyone must learn each other's names regardless of the size of the class, whether it's a seminar or a larger lecture. This is the first homework: we study the roster and learn everyone's name. Later we add more information as we learn something about each person. These facts cannot be academic but rather something personal we feel comfortable sharing—"loves dogs," "has a twin," "hates onions," et cetera. (2) We read together. We read together as a class, and we create reading groups that meet outside of class. The exercise of reading together in class might sometimes be reading a poem out loud, taking turns reading a line each or breaking into small groups and going to different parts of the classroom or hallway to read out loud. Outside of the class, the reading groups meet on a weekly basis to read together the assigned material. The groups are randomly assigned and require short weekly commitments. As the semester advances, these reading groups are reconfigured so that by the end of the term everyone has read with various groups. (3) We do group projects. While there are individual reflections and papers, many of the assignments are done in groups of three to five. These are challenging at first, as students have to let go of their ways of understanding grades and authorship, but they prove rewarding. Students learn to rely on each other's strengths, hold each other accountable, and make room for each other's mistakes. All individual and collective assignments are peer-reviewed, all writing begins with workshops, and students slowly learn to become invested in collective learning, as the philosophy of the classroom demands we accompany each other and make it together to the end of the term. In a society that constantly urges people to *have more*, Tomlinson and Lipsitz remind us that the real task is to learn how to *be more*.[17] Collective learning teaches us how to be more through accompanying others.

In fall 2018, I taught a course entitled Diaspora Archives. The entire course revolved around the collective construction of an alternative digital archive grounded in oral interviews and multimedia texts. We had the pleasure of working with Black Italian activist and filmmaker Medhin Paolos throughout the semester. She guided us in learning how to listen to and hold stories. Students worked in groups of five, following thematic guidelines and using a set of oral interviews that had been collected by myself and a group of students in a previous course as a model for their research to continue the work that their peers had started. The class was composed of graduate students, advanced undergraduates, and two first-year undergraduate students (the groups were balanced accordingly). In addition to reading critical archival studies theory and learning about methodologies of research and oral histories, students worked on providing a historical framework and evidence about the person they focused on. We all contributed equally. The projects and the class were particularly successful because students were able to tap into their own personal interests and experiences as they approached their topics. Each group had a research leader with a personal connection to the archive they developed. One group, for instance, worked on a project they titled "Birthing across Borders," which centered around the life of Doña Ofelia, a woman who crossed the US-Mexico border to birth her two daughters and found herself entangled in a long legal battle with the California medical system. The group, led by doctoral candidate Adrián Ríos, who was born on the border and grew up around women who practice border-crossing for childbirth, created an archive that documented birthing across borders historically and legally. Centering on Doña Ofelia the group mapped a history of birthing across borders that showed how long this practice has existed in the different sites and communities that engage in it, the legal battles that have shaped the practice throughout the last few decades, and the class and economic disparities that color which mothers are allowed to cross borders to give birth and which are not, dismantling the narrative of the "anchor baby" through concrete comparative data, archival research, and historical mapping.[18]

Another group under the direction of student Sofia Shapiro documented the work of La Peña Gallery, a small Latina artist collective in Austin, Texas, under attack by the Marriott Corporation during the gentrification of that neighborhood that intensified in the early 2000s. Sofia had a personal connection to the gallery as her mother, who is an artist, had worked closely with it.[19] Through a grant, we were able to subsidize student travel. Thus some students, like those working on the La Peña project, traveled across the United States to Austin, some went to Mexico, Canada, and New York to conduct interviews face to face, collect data, or visit historical archives. Other groups were focused locally. One of the local groups worked on historicizing the stories of dining hall workers from Central America at Harvard who were facing possible deportation due to the end of Temporary Protected Status (TPS). All groups worked intentionally to center the stories they wanted to tell. At least one person in each group had a personal connection to the story. Their personal investment made the projects the more valuable. As leaders of the course, Paolos and I also worked on a project. Ours recovered the contributions of Dominican *guerrilleras* during the 1965 US military intervention in the Dominican Republic by focusing on the story of one woman, Yolanda.

Yolanda is a seventy-eight-year-old Dominican woman who migrated to Italy in the 1980s. I had met Yolanda, or rather, Yolanda's story through her niece, Thiara, whom I had interviewed while doing research in Italy for a book on Black Latinidad. The life of

Yolanda seems to have come out of a mythological or fantasy novel. She was the most extraordinary person I had met in life: she had been a sailor, an LGBTQ activist under a dictatorship, a guerrillera, a spy, and now in her seventies she spends her days liberating women who have been sold into prostitution. And yet, her life, her contributions to freedom were unknown outside her circle of family and friends. For the archive, Yolanda's narrative was put in the context of the 1965 Dominican civil war and US military intervention. Yolanda was a spy for the guerrilla forces fighting the US military intervention of Santo Domingo in 1965. Posing as a washer woman/sex worker, she brought contraband from the marines to the guerrilla camps. She recalls: "They would give me food in cans and cigarettes, thinking I would bring them to my family, but I would bring them to the boys who were hiding down there."[20] She also brought secret messages between camps, stole bullets and any information she could understand as she did speak some English. Had Yolanda been caught, she would have been executed on the spot. Yet, her story, and that of the many working-class women who supported the revolution and the anti-occupation forces, is not part of any official narrative. They have been erased and replaced by stories of great men, of men of war and patriots. Paolos and I set out to recover Yolanda's story and place it in larger social-historical contexts. As we did, we also found connections between her life and that of other people our students were engaging. Our archive, we soon discovered, was also a network that connected silenced histories to the people who lived them. This archive, too, was freedom.

The final projects were curated and placed in an online digital archive Paolos and I developed with support from Luke Hollis of Archimedes Digital. "Archives of Justice," as we call it, is an invitation to understand the past from the perspective of the people who experienced it and are often left out of the narrative: Black, brown, Asian, Indigenous, colonized, and migrant people—particularly those who identify as women, trans, nonbinary, and queer. Starting by simply listening to people, Archives of Justice links their stories to historical processes and events, drawing connections among sites, geographies, and human processes to help us better understand people's contributions to and participation in important moments in the contemporary history of humanity.

Historians agree that there are gaps, silences, omissions, and even lies in the official documents of the past. These gaps disproportionately erase from official narratives and archives the political interventions and legacies of women, Black, brown, Indigenous, and Asian people, immigrants, and postcolonial subjects. We invite people, then, to mind these historical gaps by listening to the stories our interview subjects entrusted us to share and engaging with the archival collections that inform and connect them to larger historical events and social movements in our modern history: civil wars, queer rights movements, global racial justice projects, African diasporas, and new patterns of Global South migration to Europe and the United States. These connections can be easily traced through an archival visualization. These links serve as an important reminder of how much we share and how we are all part of a collective human story. Students come into the classroom with a diversity of experiences and perspectives. Connecting to that rich diversity of experiences can be a powerful contradiction to the academic culture of individuality. It is a form of freedom-making that extends beyond the classroom. This type of teaching and learning gives me hope—the kind of hope philosopher Jonathan Lear calls "radical" because it encompasses the possibility of change.[21]

Teaching practices that are progressive—that ask about the work we want our work to do—allow us to confront trauma, the feeling of loss, "what slavery took away."[22] It allows both teachers and students to connect and understand what we do and why we do it. Latinx studies and other ethnic studies fields exist within a framework of radical hope as an antidote to the white supremacist, exclusionary teaching and learning that many of us are still trying to recover from. Whether we are explicit about it or not in our teaching, what we teach demands that students think of themselves as actors and relate to the reading from a personal space, from what Chicana feminist writer Cherríe Moraga calls theorizing in the flesh, which means a theory "where the physical realities of our lives—our skin color, the land or concrete we grew up on, our sexual longings—all fuse to create a politic born out of necessity."[23] When teaching Latinx students and other students of color, it becomes even more urgent to make that relationship with the text explicit, to acknowledge the affective link that exists between the subject of study and one's subject position; between theory and flesh. That acknowledgment does not distance us from a critical dialogue but rather opens the possibilities for a more sincere critique that leads to action in and out of the classroom. It allows us, as teachers, to create classroom environments that are free from violence and that guarantee the protection of the most vulnerable, where collective learning takes precedence over individual successes.

The lessons I have learned in the almost two decades I've been teaching Latinx studies transfer to both my research and my life praxis; they guide my actions and thoughts both in and out of the classroom. On a path that often pulls us in different directions (tenure, faculty meetings, national conferences, and so on), it is easy to lose sight of why we do what we do. Teaching in freedom is to be cognizant that there is a greater goal that connects us all beyond our fields, departments, and individual responsibilities: justice and equity for all human beings; it is to recognize that learning is a communal practice or, as bell hooks taught us, that learning in community is a practice of love.

4.

FINAL EXAM

Ethnic Studies as Anticolonial Method

> Any decent history of the university in the United
> States, and indeed in the Western world, will
> have to count Ethnic Studies as one of the most
> original and influential contributions of the US
> academy to the array of fields and sciences that
> constitute the modern Western university. Like-
> wise, any decent history of the university in the
> United States will have to count the academy's
> response to the constructive challenges posed by
> Ethnic Studies as one of the greatest failures of the
> US university.
>
> **—Nelson Maldonado-Torres, "Ethnic Studies
> in the Face of the Liberal Hydra"**

Ethnic studies as I practice it is a project of transformation that
seeks to decolonize the university—to challenge the ways Eurocentric knowledge about human history has been produced as

the norm, or simply as Knowledge, with a capital "K" (Literature, History, Art), while everything else (the cultures, histories, and experiences of non-Europeans) is subjugated, hidden, or silenced, portrayed as unnecessary, extracurricular, folkloric. Critical anticolonial ethnic studies includes the study of people who have been colonized, oppressed, and racialized as nonwhite: Black, Latinx, Asian, and Native. Even though the term itself is flawed (*ethnic* as a term has a colonizing and dehumanizing history that dates to the eighteenth century), in its subversive role within the university, ethnic studies centers the experiences, cultures, and histories of colonized, minoritized, nonwhite people.

As an academic field in the United States, ethnic studies is part of the larger interdisciplinary structure of American studies and in conversation with emerging fields such as decolonial studies. Ethnic studies is a rigorous transdisciplinary site for research and teaching—that is, in its research and teaching practice ethnic studies scholars could be trained in the social sciences or the humanities or both, attending to multiple methods of research. In my own work, my interdisciplinary training as an ethnic studies and American studies scholar puts me somewhere in between history and literature. The work I do then engages historical archives as well as literary texts, music, and visual arts.

The way ethnic studies functions within the academy is as a critical, anticolonial site of knowledge production, learning, and teaching. Thus it provides students, faculty, and the communities they come from with an intellectual home as well as a connection to historical and social events that shape those community experiences: colonialism, wars, migrations, and social movements. As a growing area of intellectual inquiry, ethnic studies is not only an absolute necessity; it is the only way to save academia from doom. When allowed to fulfill its purpose, ethnic studies is a praxis of justice grounded in rebellion and freedom. Given the state of our nation and our world, I cannot think of a more urgent area of study at any institution of learning from kindergarten to higher education.

What we consider to be standard curriculum, what generations of human beings who received a Western education have learned, is grounded in white supremacy but masked as objectivity. Ethnic studies is charged with filling in the immense gaps left by our Eurocentric education system, contradicting its violence, changing the narrative. As opposed to area studies (such as African studies, Asian studies, Latin American studies), which focus on national and regional territories, ethnic studies was created to challenge the already existing curriculum and focus on the history of people of various minoritized ethnicities in the United States. Over the years, these interrogations have become transnational as the linkages between colonialism, migration, and minoritized identities demand we engage with these experiences and histories beyond a particular country. Arising within the civil rights movement, as minoritized students of color demanded their histories and cultures be studied and included in the curriculum, ethnic studies also has the peculiar history of being a field of knowledge that became institutionalized through rebellion.

The first massive student mobilization demanding the establishment of an ethnic studies department took place in California in 1968–1969. Led by the Third World Liberation Front, in alliance with the Black Student Union, the Latin American Student Organization, the Asian American Political Alliance, the Phillipine American Collegiate Endeavor, and the Native American Student Union at San Francisco State College (now San Francisco State University), the five-month student strike was the longest in the history of the student revolts in our nation. It resulted in the founding of the first ethnic studies department at San Francisco State in 1969. More than the creation of a department, the biggest accomplishment of this rebellion was the national dialogue about the need to create institutional spaces of learning where subjugated knowledge and the experiences of minoritized students would be centered. Over the past half century since the creation of the San Francisco State College of Ethnic Studies, we have continued to see students rebelling, demanding, and insisting on their right to learn from a multiplicity of perspectives and histories, on the need to decolonize the university.

At many educational institutions in the United States and elsewhere, however, ethnic studies is practically nonexistent. The lack of institutional commitment to ethnic studies fields is greatly shaped by both the misunderstanding of ethnic studies as a site of so-called navel-gazing for students of color rather than a critical location of anticolonial research and teaching and a potential site of decolonial critique and activism within the university. For the small cohort of women of color faculty working within ethnic studies at Harvard during my time there, this misconception also led to the conflation of our area of studies with our racial and ethnic identities. By the logic of the university administration, both my subject position as a Black Latina and my area of study, Black Latinx studies, are one and the same. This conflation meant that other Latinx faculty not working in my field were often asked to conduct service and evaluate work in Latinx studies or to take my place as adviser to the Latinx studies program upon my departure, as was the case of a colleague in the sciences who was asked, to her surprise, to take over the advising of my humanities graduate students.

The conflation of identity with one's field of study fuels the minstrelsy and caricaturizing of our racial and ethnic identities that fulfill colonial imperatives based on white supremacist notions of who we ought to be. This became clear to the public in 2020 with the exposure of a white scholar, Jessica Krug, who pretended to be Afro Latina for years by using a fake accent and dressing herself as though she were a Black Puerto Rican from the barrio in New York

City.[1] Ironically, Krug was granted tenure and received multiple awards for her research and teaching. In my everyday life experiences on campus at Tufts, Harvard, UGA, and other institutions I have been affiliated with over the years, the expectations and white gaze projections of Latinidad manifested in the categorical dismissal of the field of knowledge that frames my work. This leads to the dismissal of students of Latinx studies who happen to also identify as Latinx—something I learned in an exchange with a colleague during my third year at Harvard. We were discussing the needs of students currently conducting research within Latinx studies; I should note that these were students of multiple ethnic and racial backgrounds interested in literatures and cultures. I was sharing how overworked I felt with nearly two dozen graduate student advisees. He asked if anyone else could take over the role, briefly going through the roster of (white) Latin American faculty working at the university in departments such as history of science and sociology. Confused, I responded that they all work in different fields. "How could they advise a dissertation in Latinx poetry and performance?" I asked. To which he responded in surprise that he assumed these were all ethnic Latinx students coming to me to discuss our shared background. He had no idea that my almost two dozen advisees were actual scholars in an actual field coming to the only person in the humanities at the university who could teach them and advise them in their studies. Stunned by his assumption, I proceeded to explain that while I indeed came from a working-class immigrant background and shared that experience with some of my students, and while some felt comfort in that shared experience, my role as their academic adviser was to provide guidance on intellectual projects in our shared field—a field that was underrepresented in every department at the university.

In her essay "Ethnic Studies Matters," Lourdes Torres writes,

We find ourselves in a paradoxical situation in ethnic studies. Despite recently celebrating over fifty years of existence in the United States, ethnic studies is still viewed by
some as a mediocre subfield or ethnic cheerleading. This
means that ethnic studies scholars not only must produce
cutting-edge research, but in many cases also must justify
their work, since review and tenure committees may still
not recognize their field as a valid area of study.[2]

The misconception of our field as nonessential and not rigorous
is based on the profound white privilege that dominates academia.
That is, the assumption that Eurocentric knowledge is the only
valid knowledge leads to misunderstanding the ethnic studies field
and its methods as invalid or, as in the case of my former colleague,
leads to the conflation of ethnic studies scholarship with the neoliberal project of diversity. (In other words, investing in ethnic studies is the same as hiring "ethnic faculty." Therefore, if we already
have ethnic faculty in other fields, we do not need to invest in ethnic studies.) The absurdity of the logic by which these decisions are
made can stem only from the absurdity of white supremacy. The
dismissal of ethnic studies as a field is a product of ignorance, white
privilege, and fear. Ethnic studies has the potential to redefine
paradigms, shift power structures, and arm students with knowledge that challenges the status quo and the colonizing project of
the university. But this potential continues to be deferred due to
inadequate institutional recognition and insufficient or obstructed
access to regimes of academic respectability. Supporting ethnic
studies means relinquishing some (white) privilege and power.
That is not something universities will do without a fight.

Writing at the turn of the twentieth century, Black Puerto
Rican scholar and bibliophile Arthur Schomburg advocated for the
creation of departments of Black history and for Black people to

become historians. He believed that in doing so, Black and brown people could contest the lies, silence, and outright violence of the university. His proposal reintroduced "what slavery took away": the possibility of humanity and belonging.[3] Ethnic studies privileges those who have been left out of books, people who by virtue of white supremacy are made to feel (and are treated as) less than human, less capable, less worthy of study. What could possibly be a more important goal for a teacher and a learning institution?

Yet, over the years, and in particular as I entered the tenure track, my ethnic studies praxis—founding Freedom University, engaging in public acts of civil disobedience that led to my arrests, my work with queer people of color communities, my commitment to Haitian rights in the Dominican Republic—has often been met with both caution and trepidation by colleagues and well-meaning advisers. Many ask, *Should you wait until you have tenure to be so vocal about X, Y, Z? Is it safe for you to be so open about your politics in the classroom?* While I would have loved to have dismissed these questions, the increased violations of academic freedom that left some of my ethnic studies colleagues out of work or otherwise hindered their careers through tenure denials and the like were simply too many to ignore.[4]

The cautionary tales and well-meaning advice reflect the widely accepted idea that while professors are expected to be politically engaged and informed, there needs to be a clear separation between said engagement and their research and teaching in order to maintain academic integrity and a sense of objectivity. But how do we separate our teaching from our practices when the communities we study and serve are under attack? How do we, as Latinx, ethnic studies, and anticolonial teachers, study the historical violence experienced by our communities while simultaneously staying silent as families are separated at borders, people are deported, young people go to prison, schools are defunded, neighborhoods are gentrified, and Black people are murdered? Don't we, as scholars and teachers, have a responsibility to "work for justice," as bell hooks urges us to do?[5] To work toward returning a little of "what slavery took away," as Schomburg invited us to do? Education, the arts, and the humanities have always been sites of sociopolitical engagement, in part due to the freedom of creativity they afford us and in part because the arts, education, and social justice programs are often the first institutional sites to feel the effects of neoliberal politics (budget cuts, personnel reductions, et cetera). And yet, I also understand that commitment to social justice, whether it is in the classroom, in the community, or in grassroots organizing, has many faces. Commitment to social justice—activism—emerges from a deeply personal place that is not always named. Therefore, my intention here is not to invite teachers to be "activists" but to provide a method for engaging social justice in the classroom. I share some of the deeply personal lessons I have learned in my own crooked *vaivén* (coming and going) through teaching Latinx studies in the multiple and very different institutions and classrooms I have inhabited over the years. I invite you to think about the possibilities that can emerge if we foreground social justice as a clear goal in our teaching, if we think through the tools that ethnic studies provides.

Ethnic studies brings forth silenced knowledge, all the stories and histories that have not been privileged as the norm or as objective truth: this includes the perspectives of Indigenous populations on processes of colonization; views about republicanism and citizenship from the perspectives of people who have been excluded from the nation, and critics of capitalism that understand it as a racial system of oppression. Many of us have been deprived of a proper education because we've been brought up with partial, very limited views of the world and with some ideas of truth—what we think happened, what we feel certain about—that are incomplete, biased, and racialized. When we talk about processes like independence, revolution, the birth of a nation, the women's rights movement, major literary and cultural movements, the environment, and human progress, we think we have the right dates, the proper names of the people who created those nations or led those movements, or who invented those advancements. We think we know the cause and effects of social events affecting our world. We have constitutions that become the universal truths about particular nations with seemingly inclusive language like "all men are created equal," language written at a moment in which slavery was still legal and in which women did not count as full human beings. All official history is no more than partial truths, pieces of stories told as remembered by those who had the right to do so. What hasn't made it into the official archives or the textbooks—the footnotes in the official narratives, the perspectives that are often considered subjective, the theory of the flesh—that is knowledge ethnic studies is concerned with centering.

I teach my students to question everything they read, to identify the silences even in my own syllabus and in my lectures, to ask about the silences even if we do not yet know how to fill them. To notice the absences and the omission. And to name and locate the position from which knowledge is being written and produced. For all that claims to be objective and truthful exists because of that which it silences. And it is those silences that we truly need to understand about our collective human experience. There are all these other narratives out there, all these other versions of history, all this amazing art that we must see. They have been hidden, purposely or not, and what we try to do in ethnic studies is resurface them and question the forces that produced their exclusion.

Many of us have had the experience of learning history, art, and philosophy through the lens of the US Empire. From the moment our children go to school in kindergarten until they reach college, what we mean by "education" comes from a very small subset of our humanity: the version of our humanity that has dominated, oppressed, and colonized the rest of us. What we teach, what we think of as legitimate knowledge, what we uphold as having value, and what we consider our sacred canons are grounded in the dominance of whiteness and the colonial structures that engendered American universities. Ethnic studies contradicts the dominance of white supremacy in education. It opens the possibility for students to see things through a different lens than the one they were given and question what they were told was truth.

Schomburg was an idealist and an entrepreneur who very much believed in the possibility of freedom and equality for all people. When he migrated to New York City at the end of the nineteenth century, he did so because he wanted to join the revolutionary efforts to free Puerto Rico from Spanish colonial exploitation. In New York, however, he soon found himself in the "belly of the beast," to borrow José Martí's famous phrase, as US colonialism swallowed up Puerto Rico and spat him out as a noncitizen migrant—as a different kind of Black man. It was hard enough to be a Black man in the world, but to be a Black migrant was a challenge that did not even have a name yet; we did not then have words like *diaspora* and *Latinidad*. Despite his incredible success, Schomburg always lived in between two forms of unbelonging: Black and migrant. Although Schomburg did not define himself as an Afro Latino or Latinx (again, these terms were not available to him at the turn of the twentieth century), his experience with race, migration, and unbelonging are relevant to many of us who identify as Black or brown Latinx people today. Whether born in the US or elsewhere, our racialized bodies, our Hispanic last names, our accents, and our immigrant experiences continue to exclude many of us from Americanness: We are Latinx, Latina/o, and in this country, in this political climate, that is a mark of unbelonging and exclusion.

Reading Schomburg's work, however, one cannot help but feel a flash of optimism and hope. This man was ahead of his time. He articulated Black diaspora before the term existed. As early as 1901, he connected the dots between US colonialism in the Pacific and the Caribbean, marking that it produced second-class citizenship. He saw that the only way to a future of "racial integrity" was through transnational forms of anticolonial solidarity grounded in knowledge, history, and the possibility of another way of learning. Schomburg wrote,

> The white scholar's mind and heart are fired because in the temple of learning they are told how on March 5, 1770, the Americans were able to beat the English; but to find Crispus Attucks it is necessary to go deep into special books. . . .[6] Where is our historian to give us our side of view? We need in the coming dawn the man who will give us *the background of our future*; it matters not whether he comes from the cloisters of the university or from the rank and file of the fields.[7]

Schomburg dedicated his life to building the world's largest archive of Black histories and left it there for us to build upon, to write books with and about, to teach from, to fuel Black scholars' minds. His life's work, his archive, was built with the hope that we would grab the torch and keep moving. Some of us have tried.

Over the past almost two decades of teaching Latinx studies at various institutions—Dartmouth College, the University of Georgia, Harvard University, Freedom University, and Tufts University—I have seen what Schomburg meant by "kindling the torches" of knowledge that would "inspire us to racial integrity."[8] Semester after semester, as my courses fill with first-generation, mostly Latinx students of various racial, national, and economic backgrounds, I marvel at how reading, thinking, and producing work through the frameworks of anticolonial Latinx and ethnic studies empowers them. The dozens of letters and emails from students over these years saying things like "This class saved me" or "Reading Josefina Báez changed my life" have been tangible reminders of the importance of doing anticolonial Latinx, Black, and ethnic studies work—not only in terms of building the "background of the future" and "kindling the torches" of knowledge, as Schomburg hoped we would, but also in creating spaces for survival and community within the colonial, violent structures of higher education that continue to portray Latinx lives, knowledge, faculty, and students as nonessential, as extras in the perfectly orchestrated machinery of the corporate university system.

Scholar P. Gabrielle Foreman argues that ethnic studies "emerges from a necessary history of organizing as well as scholarly and pedagogical rigor and institution building. And its genealogies and teleologies may lead us" to boycott and to rebellion. Responding to my tenure denial and, by extension, Harvard's disavowal of ethnic studies, she suggested, "If Harvard is so clearly marking the body of our work as foreign and unwanted, it may be time to suspend a long and unequal relationship and to withhold our labor: no rankings and reviews, no letters of recommendation for its graduate or fellowship programs. That may be one way in which Ethnic Studies and its aligned, maligned, fields of Black Studies, Indigenous Studies, Caribbean Studies, and Latinx Studies, matter powerfully today."[9] This is also one way ethnic studies can be a project of rebellion.

Teaching Ethnic Studies in Pandemic Time

The COVID-19 pandemic brought to light a multiplicity of crises: the fragility of capitalism, the precariousness of our medical system, the inadequacy of our public health system, and the insufficiency of social services. Universities have not been immune to the effects of the COVID-19 pandemic. As part of the corporate capitalist machinery, universities have seen many losses all too quickly. Hiring has been frozen, workers laid off, student financial aid cut, and we are all bracing ourselves for the worst that is yet to come. Still, as they face financial stress, universities continue to assure students that the integrity of their education will be preserved—that knowledge-making and learning will continue. At Harvard, where I created and directed the Latinx Secondary, a graduate student certificate that currently serves twenty-four students from across the university, I saw these impacts up close. Years of neglect of Latinx studies, paired with tenure denials, inability to retain Latinx faculty, and the freeze on hiring left my students in a precarious position without a structured Latinx studies program, despite the university's commitment to "excellence in learning and teaching." Likewise, across the United States, hiring searches in ethnic studies and Latinx studies have been canceled or put on hold. No one protests. We say nothing. We are in crisis and there is nothing that we can do. Students must adapt, study something else, or find a way to learn on their own. Teach themselves their own histories. People are dying, and Latinx studies is nonessential.

Except it is essential.

Through the lens and the framework of ethnic studies, future doctors, lawyers, teachers, public servants, and businesspeople learn a more ethical, more just way to live, create, and serve one another. What could possibly be more essential to our humanity as the very people centered in ethnic studies are sent to the front lines of our society—be it in the pandemic, in a war, or in the fields, to be sacrificed, to do the work the privileged will not? What could possibly be more essential to our universities than to provide the opportunity for learning about this crisis from the very experiences of those who are most affected by it, from the knowledge that comes from, as Schomburg put it, the "rank and file of the fields"?

Before COVID-19 hit the US in March 2020, college students across the country were mobilizing in support of ethnic studies, demanding better conditions for graduate students and protesting racism, misogyny, and inequality. At Harvard, students were demanding ethnic studies programs and courses and clarity around tenure denials of professors of color, including my own. On the other side of the country, at Stanford University, students were asking, "Who is teaching us?" to raise awareness about the lack of faculty diversity on campus. At Yale, students were demanding the departmentalization of ethnic studies, faculty resources, and clarity around the tenure denial of Latinx studies faculty. The list could go on and on, well beyond the Ivy League. In 2019, as we celebrated the fiftieth anniversary of the creation of the first ethnic studies program at San Francisco State University, other schools were and still are fighting to retain a single faculty member devoted to ethnic studies scholarship, to hire a second person, or to create at least a minor in the field. All these requests go unmet by institutions because, like our people, our field is considered nonessential.

As I experienced the disavowal of Latinx studies (and by extension, ethnic studies) at the institution where I'd worked to build it for eight years, I returned to Schomburg's call for "kindling the torches of knowledge"—for building departments and programs, teaching against the white supremacy of the university even if from within the belly of the beast. I continue to wonder, where did we go wrong? How are we, one hundred years later, *still* having this fight? Why do we *still* need to convince our institutions that this knowledge is essential, that our students matter, that our work has value?

Dylan Rodriguez said it best: "[Ethnic Studies] represents some of the most transformative, epistemologically, and theoretically challenging, critically and publicly engaged work to emerge from the academy in the last half century. In producing such field- and academy-altering work, Ethnic Studies represents the elite research university's (e.g., Harvard et al.'s) antithesis."[10] How can the university reward and support a field whose very purpose is to dismantle the structures on which the institution is grounded? Like Schomburg and his project of diasporic blackness at the turn of the twentieth century, Latinx studies and ethnic studies live within the belly of the beast. As scholars in these fields, we produce knowledge, create spaces, and teach in contradiction with the colonial, oppressive structures of the white supremacist university. Our work, our people, our students are regurgitated and spat out if we are not subtle enough, if we upset the belly, if our work becomes too essential. So, where do we go from here? How do we continue amid this violence? How do we rebel, and how do we win?

One of Schomburg's most incredible propositions was that of "a nation without a nation," a concept we now understand as diaspora. For Schomburg, however, this nation of transnational solidarity did not mean he gave up his place within the US nation.[11] He strived to create an alternative place of belonging as he continued to make space for himself amid the discomfort. We need to do the same. We must also create our own nations without nations, our own institutions without institutions, our own freedom schools within the institutions, our collectives of *duras* to protect us. When I write and teach, I do so in contradiction with the institution I work for and against the fields that I write through. I worked for eight years at an institution that justified the denial of Puerto Rican citizenship, that supported intervention in the Dominican Republic based on the logic of scientific racism, and that was built on stolen land by enslaved Black people. But that is what the project of the university was. Universities were created for the sons of rich colonizers to continue the colonial project and, eventually, the national project that was always based on colonial regimes of racial and economic exclusion. Coming into a university as a woman of color, a descendant of enslaved people, and an immigrant is already a disruption of that system. The whole point of my work is to contradict the university as it is and as it was imagined, and not everyone is on board with that project. Many people benefit from white supremacy and from policing the borders of knowledge-making. It takes a lot of courage and awareness to step up and say, "We know the structures of this institution are racist, we know we benefit from that structure and have been complicit in sustaining it, but we want to change that"—and then actually do that structural work. It takes *ganas*, commitment, and sacrifice. Very few people benefiting from this system want to do more than pay lip service to the fight against white supremacist systems that allow them to thrive and succeed at the expense, exploitation, discouragement, and disavowal of their nonwhite colleagues.

What, then, can we do to decolonize the university? What does that work look like? I do not have all the answers. I do know that there are things we can do to start, like hiring faculty of color who come from communities that have been oppressed and underprivileged. That means taking the research of these scholars seriously, valuing it, amplifying it, and supporting it. That means not exploiting faculty of color by demanding unbearable amounts of service. That means promoting faculty of color, retaining them, rewarding them for the extra labor they produce, and granting them tenure. It also means rethinking and abolishing the corporate ties of the institutions, divesting from prisons and fossil fuels. It means building centers, institutes, and departments that center subjugated knowledge across fields. It means having a practical plan for supporting first-generation students, students with DACA and undocumented students, and BIPOC and LGBTQ+ students. It means understanding that the project of "diversity and inclusion" has failed. It means making social justice and equality the most important goals in every space of the institution, from the classrooms and dining halls to the dean's office. That requires shifting gears from a reactive to a proactive approach—from simply condemning racism in a memo to constructing spaces and programs that are antiracist and anticolonial and that actively combat white supremacy.

What would the ideal university look like?

It would look like a group of scholars of all races and ethnicities centering the work, histories, and artistic production of marginalized, minoritized, and colonized Black, Latinx, Asian, Indigenous, immigrant, disabled, and queer people rather than viewing them as objects of study. That should not only be the domain of ethnic studies; it should be the work of the whole university. We should be thinking about the dismantling of white supremacy in our institutions and the recentering of subjugated knowledge everywhere, in every department. Or maybe get rid of departments altogether and start thinking about relevant questions rather than strict disciplines, to start answering the questions that we've been musing over for the past two hundred years through other lenses, other knowledges, and other literatures. Let's see where that gets us.

In the meantime, we must continue to rebel through our research and our praxis of thinking and doing ethnic studies, creating our own pockets of freedom in our classrooms, our communities of sustenance and belonging. We must continue to sing against the aggressors and oppressors as did my great-grandmother Julia, to unite in protest, and to rebel in community.

La lucha sigue.

ACKNOWLEDGMENTS

I wrote this little book during one of the most trying times of my life, in the wake of the tenure denial that upended my life and as the world shut down due to the COVID-19 pandemic. Writing this book was my own act of radical hoping. It was also a gesture of gratitude for the solidarity and kindness I received from so many people across the globe: friends and family, colleagues and students, and people I have never met. For every hateful act I endured, a dozen acts of kindness followed. This gave me hope. This made it possible for me to wake up every morning and write. So first and foremost, I want to thank the almost six thousand people who signed petitions, wrote letters, and sent notes of encouragement as I faced this violence, the dozens of students who sustained months of active protests and civil disobedience calling for ethnic studies at Harvard until the pandemic forced them to stop, and the creators of and contributors to the Ethnic Studies Rise initiative and "Lorgia Fest," especially Katerina González Seligmann, Alex Gil, and Raj Chetty. While I was unable to respond to each message, or individually thank each of you, I read everything and treasured every word. Your kindness was my salvation, and I will forever be grateful to you.

I owe my survival to my Boston crew of *duras*, the badass womxn who sustained me these past two years—your love and care are the best of all gifts. Thank you, Medhin Paolos, Durba Mitra,

Genevieve Clutario, Irene Mata, Lauren Kaminsky, Paola Ibarra, Jodi Rosenbaum, and Kirsten Weld for making Boston hospitable for me despite all my wounds. Many dear *amigas* and *comadres* near and far nourished me with words, food, and *mimos*: Josefina Báez, Sharina Maillo-Pozo, Pam Voekel, Beth Manley, Dana Bultman, Bethany Moreton, Betina Kaplan, Eric Gómez, Heijin Lee, Afia Ofori-Mensa, and Adnaloy Espinosa were so present, despite their geographical distance, that I could almost feel their arms embracing me through the phone or screen. Chandra Talpade-Mohanty, Angela Y. Davis, P. Gabrielle Foreman, Alicia Schmidt Camacho, and Yolanda Martínez-San Miguel offered advice and talked me through multiple options as I contemplated unemployment in pandemic times. The time you invested in me, your worries for my well-being, your support of not just my career but my person, was my sustenance.

Many of my students became family these past few years, sharing not only our communal desire to change academia but also laughter, food, and beautiful moments of quiet resistance. I want to acknowledge especially Alondra Ponce, Massiel Torres Ulloa, and Keish Kim, for building this feminist warrior family with me in Boston. Your work and your fire fuel my radical hope for another way of doing this work, together.

I wrote this book for and because of women in my life, women in my history and ancestry, and for women I will never meet but who are very much part of me. It has been because of this community of women and a few cis-men allies that I have been able to do the work I do. I would like to acknowledge George Lipsitz, Silvio Torres-Saillant, Cornel West, Satya Mohanty, Robin D. G. Kelley, Dean Saranillio, and Walter Johnson, whose kindness, friendship, and support have been the most wonderful of gifts.

Many thanks to Teresita Fernández for cheering me on as I wrote and for giving me the gift of her beautiful art for the cover; to

Dao Tran for her incisive editorial work that ultimately made this book more accessible to readers, to Anthony Arnove for believing in this project and seeing it to fruition, to Yarimar Bonilla for directing me to Haymarket Books, to Maaza Mengiste, Barbara Ransby, Deborah Paredez, Achy Obejas, and Megan Bayles for reading the manuscript and providing feedback, comments, and supportive blurbs. Chapter 3 grew out of a shorter piece I wrote for a collection of essays entitled *Critical Dialogues in Latinx Studies*, edited by Ana Ramos-Zayas and Mérida Rúa. I feel grateful for the *diálogo* that space provided to think about liberation and community as praxis.

Finally, my eternal gratitude to my grandmother Altagracia Franjul, for fanning the fire that led me to this path of community and rebellion. *Gracias*.

NOTES

1. Course Objective: On Being "The One"

1.	While there is no quantitative research on tenure denials of controversial faculty, over the last decade, public exposés in the media and social media have brought attention to the practice. Most notable are the recent cases of scholar-journalist Nikole Hannah-Jones, who was denied tenure by the University of North Carolina, and of philosopher Cornel West denied tenure by Harvard. See Katie Robertson, "Nikole Hannah-Jones Denied Tenure at University of North Carolina," *New York Times*, May 19, 2021, www.nytimes. com/2021/05/19/business/media/nikole-hannah-jones-unc.html; Julia Lieblich, "Harvard's History of Inscrutable Tenure Denials," *Nation*, March 9, 2021, www.thenation.com/article/society/harvard-tenure-cornel-west/.

2.	Nathan Matias, Neil Lewis Jr., and Elan Hope, "Universities Say They Want More Diverse Faculties. So Why Is Academia Still So White?" FiveThirty-Eight, September 7, 2021, https://fivethirtyeight.com/features /universities-say-they-want-more-diverse-faculties-so-why-is-academia -still-so-white/. See also "Tenure" in the "Issues" section of the American Association of University Professors website, www.aaup.org/issues/tenure.

3.	The 2011 United States Department of Education Employees by Assigned Position survey reports that out of the more than 1.5 million members of the academic workforce, 1.1 million (or roughly 73 percent) were teaching off the tenure track in temporary or contingent appointments. See David Laurence, "A Profile of the Non-Tenure-Track Academic Workforce," *ADFL Bulletin* 42, no. 3 (2013): 6–22, https://doi.org/10.1632/adfl.42.3.6. See also National Center for Education Statistics Report on 2020–2021 faculty salary.

4.	While there were a handful of tenured Latinx professors (who did not work in Latinx or Ethnic Studies) at Harvard during my time there, I was the only untenured Latina at the time. The majority of people the university identify as Latinx, I should note, were white Latin American or Spanish. I was one of two Afro Latina professors in the entire university.

5.   Sara Ahmed, *On Being Included: Racism and Diversity in Institutional Life* (Durham, NC: Duke University Press, 2012), 5.

6.   When I use the term "elite university," I am referring to Ivy League and private prestigious schools with highly competitive admissions processes and large endowments.

7.   Yolanda Flores Niemann, Gabriella Gutiérrez y Muhs, and Carmen G. González, introduction to *Presumed Incompetent II: Race, Class, Power, and Resistance of Women in Academia*, eds. Yolanda Flores Niemann, Gabriella Gutiérrez y Muhs, and Carmen G. González (Boulder: University Press of Colorado, 2020), 3.

8.   Ahmed, *On Being Included*, 3.

9.   See Amelia N. Gibson, "Civility and Structural Precarity for Faculty of Color in LIS," *Journal of Education for Library and Information Science* 60, no. 3 (2019): 215–22; Julian Vasquez Heilig et al., "Considering the Ethnoracial and Gender Diversity of Faculty in United States College and University Intellectual Communities." *Hisp. JL & Pol'y* (2019): 1; Isis H. Settles, Martinique K. Jones, NiCole T. Buchanan, and Kristie Dotson, "Epistemic Exclusion: Scholar(ly) Devaluation That Marginalizes Faculty of Color," *Journal of Diversity in Higher Education* (2020).

10.   Lourdes Torres, "Ethnic Studies Matters," *Kalfou* 7, no. 2 (2020): 215–21.

11.   As I discuss in chapter 4, while ethnic studies has been an established field for half a century, and while schools on the West and East Coasts (particularly in California, New York, and New Jersey) have established ethnic studies programs, at times divided by regional ethnic differences such as Puerto Rican studies in New York and Chicano studies in Los Angeles, in the New England region, schools have resisted institutionalization of ethnic studies programs despite student demand since the late 1970s. The creation of the Latina/o Studies Program at Williams College in 2014; the Ethnic Studies Program at Wellesley in 2014; the Program in Ethnicity, Migration, and Race at Yale; and the Department of Studies in Race, Colonialism, and Diaspora at Tufts, among many other student-led initiatives, are leading a major shift not only in where ethnic studies is taught but also in the way it engages with intersectional fields and with global concerns about justice and equity.

12.   According to the National Center for Education Statistics, as of 2018 about 75 percent of full-time faculty are white. Black and Latinx women account for a meager 3 percent. See https://nces.ed.gov/fastfacts/display.asp?id=61.

13.   Robin D. G. Kelley, "Black Study, Black Struggle," *Ufahamu: A Journal of African Studies* 40, no. 2 (2018): 153–68 (originally published in 2016 in the *Boston Review*).

14.   Ramona Hernández, "The Legacy of Dominicanidad," a symposium

honoring the work of Lorgia García Peña, Harvard University, Thursday, January 30, 2020, https://hutchinscenter.fas.harvard.edu/event /legacy-dominicanidad-symposium-work-lorgia-garcía-peña.

15. National Center for Education Statistics, "Race and Ethnicity of College Faculty,"https://nces.ed.gov/fastfacts/display.asp?id=61.

16. National Center for Education Statistics, "Race and Ethnicity of College Faculty."

17. bell hooks, *Killing Rage: Ending Racism* (New York: Henry Holt, 1996), 265.

18. In *The Borders of Dominicanidad* (Duke University Press, 2016), I introduce the term contra*diction* to think about alternative narratives, stories, and archives that can help us think about possibilities beyond or against hegemonic versions of history.

19. Camara Brown, "The Intimacy They Were Looking For: Black Women Theorizing Feminism and Friendship, 1901–1988," dissertation prospectus in American Studies, Harvard University, December 9, 2020.

20. Lorgia García-Peña, *The Borders of Dominicanidad: Race, Nation, and Archives of Contradiction* (Durham, NC: Duke University Press, 2016).

21. Ginetta E. B. Candelario, *Black behind the Ears: Dominican Racial Identity from Museums to Beauty Shops* (Durham, NC: Duke University Press, 2007).

22. Kelley, "Black Study, Black Struggle," 161–62.

23. Kelley, "Black Study, Black Struggle," 162.

24. Ahmed, *On Being Included*, 66.

25. Gloria Anzaldúa, *The Gloria Anzaldúa Reader*, ed. AnaLouise Keating (Durham, NC: Duke University Press, 2009), 204–5.

26. Colleen Flaherty, "Outspoken Out of a Job?" *Inside Higher Ed*, December 17, 2020, www.insidehighered.com/news/2020/12/17/scholars-pledge-not-speak-ole-miss-until-it-reinstates-colleague.

27. Flores Niemann, Gutiérrez y Muhs, and González, introduction to *Presumed Incompetent II*, 5.

2. Reading List: Complicity with Whiteness Will Not Save You

1. I use "knowledges" in plural to account for the plurality and diversity of the intellectual, historical, and cultural meanings that come from the various communities embodied in the umbrella term "people of color."

2. National Center for Education Statistics, "Race and Ethnicity of College Faculty."

3. Grace Park, "My Tenure Denial," in *Presumed Incompetent II*, 280.

4. Joanne Trejo, "The Burden of Service for Faculty of Color to Achieve

Diversity and Inclusion: The Minority Tax," *Molecular Biology of the Cell* 31, no. 25 (November 2020): https://doi.org/10.1091/mbc.E20-08-0567. Over the past five years we have seen a growth in studies about the impact of the "minority tax" on various academic fields, including medicine, the sciences, social sciences, and the humanities. See, for example, Kendall M. Campbell and José E. Rodríguez, "Addressing the Minority Tax: Perspectives from Two Diversity Leaders on Building Minority Faculty Success in Academic Medicine," *Academic Medicine* 94, no. 12 (2019): 1854–57, and, José E. Rodríguez, Maria Harsha Wusu, Tanya Anim, Kari-Claudia Allen, and Judy C. Washington, "Abolish the Minority Woman Tax!" *Journal of Women's Health* 30, no. 7 (2021): 914–15.

5.   "Maria," in conversation with the author via teleconference (Zoom), March 1, 2020.

6.   "Maria," in conversation with the author, March 1, 2020.

7.   "Maria," in conversation with the author, March 1, 2020.

8.   See "FAS Dean Gay Declares 'Institutional Commitment' to Ethnic Studies in Wake of Protests," *The Crimson*, December 10, 2019, www.thecrimson.com/article/2019/12/10/ethnic-studies-concentration.

9.   "Jane," in conversation with the author, April 12, 2020 (via phone).

10. "Jane," in conversation with the author, April 12, 2020.

11. "Jane," in conversation with the author, April 12, 2020.

12. Esther O. Ohito, "Some of Us Die: A Black Feminist Researcher's Survival Method for Creatively Refusing Death and Decay in the Neoliberal Academy." *International Journal of Qualitative Studies in Education* (2020): 1–19, 5.

13. Latinx faculty meeting, author's notes, April 6, 2021.

14. Christina Sharpe, *In the Wake: On Blackness and Being* (Durham, NC: Duke University Press, 2016).

15. Kent Jason G. Cheng, Yue Sun, and Shannon M. Monnat, "COVID-19 Death Rates Are Higher in Rural Counties with Larger Shares of Blacks and Hispanics," *Journal of Rural Health* 36, no. 4 (2020): 602–8.

3. Midterm: Teaching as Accompaniment

1.   See Elizabeth S. Manley, "Of Celestinas and Saints, or Deconstructing the Myths of Dominican Womanhood." *Small Axe: A Caribbean Journal of Criticism* 22, no. 2 (2018): 72–84, 76, and *The Paradox of Paternalism: Women and the Politics of Authoritarianism in the Dominican Republic* (Gainesville: University Press of Florida, 2017) for a more complete examination of Dominican feminism in the twentieth century.

2.   Policy 4.1.6, "Admission of Persons Not Lawfully Present in the United
      States," and Policy 4.3.4, "Verification of Lawful Presence" in Board of
      Regents Policy Manual (2010). Official Policies of the University System of
      Georgia, www.usg.edu/policymanual/section4/policy/4.1_general_policy/.
3.   Nicole Guidotti-Hernández, "Old Tactics, New South," *Ms. Magazine*,
      November 16, 2011, https://msmagazine.com/2011/11/16/old-tactics-
      new-south/.
4.   Azadeh Shahshahani, "HB 87 Negatively Impacts Georgia Economy and
      Reputation," *Jurist*, May 18, 2012, www.jurist.org/commentary/2012/05/
      azadeh-shahshahani-georgia-hb87/.
5.   Jonathan Lear, *Radical Hope: Ethics in the Face of Cultural Devastation*
      (Cambridge, MA: Harvard University Press, 2006).
6.   bell hooks, "Teaching Community: A Pedagogy of Hope," *Psychology Press*
      36 (2003): xiii.
7.   I wrote about Performing Latinidad in "Bridging Activism and Teaching in
      Latinx Studies," in *Critical Dialogues in Latinx Studies: A Reader*, ed. Ana Y.
      Ramos-Zayas and Mérida M. Rúa (New York: NYU Press, 2021).
8.   I was appointed to teach Latinx studies, but there is no Latinx studies
      department. Instead, I teach my courses within existing departments (Ro-
      mance Languages and Literature, American Studies, and so forth).
9.   From the time I began teaching at Harvard in 2013 to my departure in 2021,
      the student body became more diverse, particularly as the administration
      strengthened its commitment to admitting first-generation minority stu-
      dents. An unintended effect of this has been student activism in support of
      custodial and dining-hall workers, whom first-generation students of color
      often perceive as close friends—or as one student put it, "family."
10.   Mathew Rodriguez, "Latino Donald Trump Supporter Says More Mexi-
      cans Means a Taco Truck on Every Corner," *Mic*, September 2, 2016, www.
      mic.com/articles/153367/latino-donald-trump-supporter-says-more-mex-
      icans-means-a-taco-truck-on-every-corner#.2DujMnmZJ.
11.   The Harvard University campus receives hundreds of tourists per week
      who visit the yard and line up to take pictures with the Harvard statue.
      During the performance, many of the tourists became part of the action—
      some knowingly, others accidentally.
12.   Barbara Tomlinson and George Lipsitz, "American Studies as Accompani-
      ment," *American Quarterly* 65, no. 1 (March 2013): 1–30.
13.   Tomlinson and Lipsitz, "American Studies as Accompaniment," 9–10.
14.   The petition, which can still be found on google docs via the PUSH Facebook
      page (https://docs.google.com/forms/d/e/1FAIpQLSemp4Jd77TAlkWz-
      vcc_dxZSm9sfiEm3lUM2KMqC1IBlyGgx1w/viewform?c=0&w=1&fb-

clid=IwAR2CnfIWXibbb6-OTu3ENb0I1dmtF8sdpW55Mp65raB0n86_Ks-bQBnQEImY), states: "In admitting students from at-risk and marginalized communities, Harvard has the obligation to provide these members of our community with an equitable and just education, which requires the creation of spaces and the allocation of resources that support them and allow them to excel at Harvard University and beyond. Harvard prides itself on its diversity and inclusivity; let's then support our diverse population in this hour of increased fear and need" and lists a series of demands including a physical space, funds, and mental health support for undocumented students.

Four of the students enrolled in the class wrote a piece for the *Harvard Crimson*, the student newspaper, entitled "Pushing Harvard Towards Sanctuary," published on November 30, 2016, in which they highlight their demands and the reasons for asking the university to create a sanctuary for its undocumented students, www.thecrimson.com/article/2016/11/30/-harvard-push-response-to-Faust/. For more on PUSH or to access their archives, see https://www.facebook.com/PUSHarvard/.

15. See Stephen Santa-Ramirez, "A Historical Snapshot of Latinx Student Activism from the 1960s to 1990s: A University Archival Analysis," *Journal of Hispanic Higher Education* (April 2021), https://journals.sagepub.com/doi/abs/10.1177/15381927211008681.

16. Letter from student, Black Latinidad course, Tufts University, December 2021.

17. Tomlinson and Lipsitz, "American Studies as Accompaniment."

18. See "Doña Ofelia" in Archives of Justice, https://archivesofjustice.org/.

19. Shapiro developed a website for this project, https://sofiashapiro.wixsite.com/latinaartaustin.

20. See "Yolanda" in Archives of Justice, https://archivesofjustice.org/.

21. Lear, *Radical Hope*, 12.

22. Arthur A. Schomburg, "The Negro Digs Up His Past (1925)," in *The New Negro: Readings on Race, Representation, and African American Culture* 1938 (1892): 326–29, 326.

23. Cherríe Moraga, "Entering the Lives of Others. A Theory in the Flesh," in *This Bridge Called My Back*, ed. Gloria Anzaldúa and Cherríe Moraga (New York: Kitchen Table, 1981), 21.

4. Final Exam: Ethnic Studies as Anticolonial Method

1. Colleen Flaherty, "White Lies," September 4, 2020, www.insidehighered.com/news/2020/09/04/prominent-scholar-outs-herself-white-just-she-

faced-exposure-claiming-be-black.

2.   Lourdes Torres, "Ethnic Studies Matters," *Kalfou: A Journal of Comparative and Relational Ethnic Studies* 7, no. 2 (2020): 216.

3.   Schomburg, "The Negro Digs Up His Past," 326.

4.   One example is the case of American studies scholar Steven Salaita, whose tenured job offer from the University of Illinois at Urbana-Champaign was withdrawn due to a controversial tweet Salaita posted in support of Palestine.

5.   bell hooks, "Teaching Community."

6.   Crispus Attucks (c. 1723–March 5, 1770) was either an enslaved American or freeman of Wampanoag and African descent. He was the first casualty of the Boston Massacre and is widely considered the first American casualty in the American Revolutionary War.

7.   Athur Schomburg, "Racial Integrity: A Plea for the Establishment of a Chair of Negro History in Our Schools and Colleges," address delivered at the Teachers' Summer Class at the Cheney Institute, Pennsylvania, July 1913, 68.

8..   Schomburg, "Racial Integrity," 68.

9.   See Katerina González Seligmann, Raj Chetty, and Alex Gil, "War on Ethnic Studies: Ethnic Studies Rising," Ethnic Studies Rise Roundtable, January 7, 2020, https://ethnicrise.github.io/roundtable/war-ethnic-studies.

10.   González Seligmann, Chetty, and Gil, "War on Ethnic Studies: Ethnic Studies Rising."

11.   Schomburg, "The Negro Digs Up His Past," 326–29.

INDEX

ABOUT HAYMARKET BOOKS

Haymarket Books is a radical, independent, nonprofit book publisher based in Chicago. Our mission is to publish books that contribute to struggles for social and economic justice. We strive to make our books a vibrant and organic part of social movements and the education and development of a critical, engaged, international left.

We take inspiration and courage from our namesakes, the Haymarket martyrs, who gave their lives fighting for a better world. Their 1886 struggle for the eight-hour day—which gave us May Day, the international workers' holiday—reminds workers around the world that ordinary people can organize and struggle for their own liberation. These struggles continue today across the globe—struggles against oppression, exploitation, poverty, and war.

Since our founding in 2001, Haymarket Books has published more than five hundred titles. Radically independent, we seek to drive a wedge into the risk-averse world of corporate book publishing. Our authors include Noam Chomsky, Arundhati Roy, Rebecca Solnit, Angela Y. Davis, Howard Zinn, Amy Goodman, Wallace Shawn, Mike Davis, Winona LaDuke, Ilan Pappé, Richard Wolff, Dave Zirin, Keeanga-Yamahtta Taylor, Nick Turse, Dahr Jamail, David Barsamian, Elizabeth Laird, Amira Hass, Mark Steel, Avi Lewis, Naomi Klein, and Neil Davidson. We are also the trade publishers of the acclaimed Historical Materialism Book Series and of Dispatch Books.

ALSO AVAILABLE FROM HAYMARKET BOOKS

Abolition. Feminism. Now.
Angela Y. Davis, Gina Dent, Erica R. Meiners, and Beth E. Richie

Angela Davis: An Autobiography
Angela Y. Davis

Assata Taught Me: State Violence, Racial Capitalism, and the Movement for Black Lives
Donna Murch

The Billboard
Natalie Y. Moore, foreword by Imani Perry

From #BlackLivesMatter to Black Liberation (Expanded Edition)
Keeanga-Yamahtta Taylor, foreword by Angela Y. Davis

Mi María: Surviving the Storm: Voices from Puerto Rico
Edited by Ricia Anne Chansky and Marci Denesiuk

Neoliberalism's War on Higher Education
Henry A. Giroux

The Sentences That Create Us: Crafting A Writer's Life in Prison
PEN America, edited by Caits Meissner, foreword by Reginald Dwayne Betts

Speaking Out of Place: Getting Our Political Voices Back
David Palumbo-Liu

ABOUT THE AUTHOR

Lorgia García Peña is a first-generation Latinx Studies scholar. Dr. García Peña is the Mellon Associate Professor of Race, Colonialism, and Diaspora Studies at Tufts University and a Casey Foundation 2021 Freedom Scholar. She studies global Blackness, colonialism, migration, and diaspora with a special focus on Black Latinidad. Dr. García Peña is the cofounder of Freedom University Georgia and of Archives of Justice (Milan-Boston). Her book *The Borders of Dominicanidad* won the 2017 National Women's Studies Association Gloria Anzaldúa Book Prize, the Isis Duarte Book Award in Haiti and Dominican Studies, and the 2016 Latino/a Studies Book Award. She is the author of *Translating Blackness* and the coeditor of the Texas University Press series Latinx: The Future Is Now. She is a regular contributor to the *Boycott Times*, *Asterix Journal*, and the North American Council on Latin America (NACLA).